Called

Called

Women in Ministry in Ireland

ANNE FRANCIS

WIPF & STOCK · Eugene, Oregon

CALLED
Women in Ministry in Ireland

Wipf & Stock
An Imprint of Wipf and Stock Publishers
199 W. 8th Ave., Suite 3
Eugene, OR 97401

www.wipfandstock.com

PAPERBACK ISBN: 978-1-6667-4235-0
HARDCOVER ISBN: 978-1-6667-4236-7
EBOOK ISBN: 978-1-6667-4237-4

06/07/22

To the Keating and Francis women.
To Brigid, Michael Éoin, and Enda.
To women in ministry.
With love.

Contents

Acknowledgments

MY SINCERE AND HEARTFELT thanks to all the women who participated in this study. My special thanks to Soline Humbert, Margaret Kiely, Heather Morris, Ruth Patterson, and Pat Storey.

My grateful thanks to Dr. Oonagh O'Brien and the Presentation Sisters who hosted the research gathering at their beautiful centre at Mount St. Anne's, Killenard.

Grateful thanks to Dr. Nicola Brady of the Irish Council of Churches and Inter-church Meeting who provided access to all member churches and who published the initial report on the ICC website.

My thanks to those denominational representatives who contacted me with information; who passed on the questionnaire to women in their churches and made valuable suggestions about avenues of enquiry: Peter Cheney (Church of Ireland), Carole Harries (Salvation Army), John McEvoy (Elim), Daphne Metcalf (Irish Theological Institute), Gillian Skillen (Methodist Church in Ireland), Jim Stothers (Presbyterian Church in Ireland), Mother Cherub Agnes Oluyinka Olushoto-Aderanti (Cherubim and Seraphim), and others who passed on the invitation informally.

Introduction

*"I don't do it because I am a woman, I do it because
I have been compelled by my vocation to seek out
the possibility of ministry in the Church."*[1]

THIS BOOK IS ABOUT women who minister. It offers a picture of their lives, concerns, call, and faithfulness in their own words. It emerges from research and reflects my experience of women in ministry over thirty-five years. I am privileged to record, curate, and honour their stories at a sensitive time in the development of women's ministry in Ireland.

The ministry of women has been present in Ireland since the early times of Christianity. Today, women's ministry is offered throughout the Christian churches. Women are presbyters, rectors, elders, and deacons in many churches. Religious sisters founded many of Ireland's healthcare centres, schools, and social projects and continue to work in spiritual and community settings. There is a female bishop in the Church of Ireland, and the Methodist Church has had a female president. Women work in various ministries, including social and pastoral ministries; music; youth and

---

1. Rev. Anne Marie O'Farrell, quoted by MacDonald "Pure Codology," 3.

1

family; spiritual accompaniment; liturgy and worship; missionary work; diocesan leadership roles; education; retreat ministry and many others.

Despite this presence and the fact that women make up a majority of churchgoers in Ireland, the ministry of women has perennially been seen as controversial. In some denominations this is embedded in rules which limit women's involvement in some ministries. In others, even where restrictions are not present, women report differences in status and experience for women and men. At this time women are neither fully integrated into ministry structures nor fully excluded. Whatever their personal gifts, calling, or ambitions, they are each managing the factor of being a woman as it is perceived in their contexts. Women are ministering at a time when their position as leaders is contested in a way that the status of their male colleagues is not.

Despite an increase in women's involvement it is still far from ordinary to be a female minister in the Christian church. As we shall see there are concerns and tensions about the future of women's ordination in the Presbyterian tradition. Archbishop Diarmuid Martin has said there is "still misogyny in the Catholic Church."[2] Times of transition will bring out convictions and tensions often concealed during more stable periods. While many voices contribute to this discussion, it is crucially important to hear the voices at its centre. It is timely to enquire into the experience of women in ministry in Ireland and to record their own views, motivations and perceptions of their way of life.

At the gathering of women which took place as part of this research I was present at an informal conversation where some ordained ministers were discussing how they should deal with the people in their congregations who objected to their ministry on the grounds that they were women. One suggested prayer, another visiting or an informal conversation after service, another suggested that time would make a difference. The tone of the conversation was entirely pastoral. None of the women dismissed or criticised those who opposed them. When faced with rejection and sexism, they dealt with it as pastors. They treated opposition on the grounds of gender as a part of everyday life.

In the early 1990s, working in a Catholic diocese, I invited other women ministering in the diocese to my house for prayer, lunch, and support. Some of us had not met before. Within thirty minutes the conversation turned to how we all coped with the behaviour of clergy colleagues. Story

2. In an interview on RTE Radio One with Miriam O'Callaghan, April 1, 2018.

after story was told about professional, experienced women being disregarded, undermined, shouted at, sexually harassed, and summarily sacked. All of this was seen as an ordinary part of the challenge of being a woman in ministry. Then in my mid-twenties I had seen enough to know that this was unremarkable. It was an occupational hazard of an otherwise rewarding and life-giving profession. One woman at that gathering said, "They didn't invite us into their church, they don't want us and they will do everything they can to get rid of us."

My experience as a woman in Christian ministry; my interaction with ministry students across the denominations, and my relationships with colleagues in ministry have given me a profound awareness of the variety of ways people experience ministry and its contexts. It is clear that each minister deals with a wide range of factors in negotiating the tasks and demands of this work, physically, mentally, spiritually, socially, and emotionally, and this in turn shapes ministry and also church communities. Female colleagues and students have always been generous in sharing their journey with me. It is clear to me that whatever they do, for good or ill, they are seen "as a woman."

OUTLINE OF THE PROJECT

This research began with simple questions. What is it like to minister as a woman in Ireland at this time? What are the joys and challenges? Is it different in different denominations or geographical regions or for those who are ordained or not? Does it matter in ministry whether the minister is male or female? What issues are most important to women who minister in Ireland? The key research question to women was *what is your experience as a female minister at this time?*

My aim was to explore the experience of women in ministry in Ireland and to identify the issues which are important. The contribution of this study is primarily an insight into this experience. From these explorations it is also possible to draw other conclusions about how women's ministry might be encouraged and supported both in particular traditions and ecumenically. In seeing how women understand and practice ministry it is possible to discern areas where understandings of ministry may adapt and grow in the light of their experience and reflection.

I chose to conduct research among women who minister across the denominational boundaries. Here areas of commonality might emerge, as well as differences among female ministers. Another reason for an ecumenical approach is Ireland's sectarian past. Doing this research across the church traditions may, in a small way, undermine sectarian thinking. While I was prepared for some of the research results to indicate denominational differences, and indeed they do, I did not want to preempt this. It is clear from the results that women in ministry have much in common, even acknowledging differences in tradition, culture, or geography.

The Scope of the Project

The Women in Ministry in Ireland Research Project had three stages. The first was a questionnaire enquiring into women's circumstances and experience of ministry.[3] This was followed by a series of interviews with female ministers falling into two categories. Fourteen were anonymous interviews with practitioners, and the remaining five were with women, also practitioners, who for various reasons have found themselves in the headlines of women's ministry in Ireland. The "Women in Ministry in Ireland" report came at the completion of these two phases and was published on the Irish Council of Churches website, January 2018.[4]

The second group of interviews, with Ruth Patterson, Heather Morris, Margaret Kiely, Soline Humbert, and Pat Storey, forms part 3 of this book. The encounters with these diverse women reveal their own rich story and also illuminate the themes which arise in the contributions of the anonymous female ministers and how they are lived out in a particular person and her context.

The third phase of the project was a gathering of women in Christian ministry who came together to discuss the findings of phases one and two. Over two days they responded to the findings of the research and raised further areas for exploration. The fruits of this discussion are summarised in chapter 4.

Methodology

This was an enquiry with an under-researched group, with the aim of exploring their experience and its implications. While their numbers and

3. Appendix 1.
4. Francis, "Women in Ministry in Ireland."

situations were of interest in providing a context, it was their experience which formed the essential data and basis for exploration. This indicated an interpretative approach which emphasised the qualitative. Interpretative phenomenological analysis rests on a "curious facilitation" of participants in sharing their experience, and I adopted this approach in conducting this research. [5] Secondly, it is my experience that the closer the methodology is to the topic, the richer the process and results.[6] As this study was conducted in a Christian ecclesial and ministerial context, I adopted an approach of *loving service*. It was my intention in conducting this research to be of some service to the participants and to the churches. I hoped that by participating in and directing this project women would feel ownership of the project and find an element of transformation in it for their own ministry.

The final phase of the research gathering reinforced the accountability and the relational nature of the project. Here, instead of my interpretation of the findings being the last word, this power was returned to the stakeholder group. This further placed women in ministry centrally in the project as they participated in a communal and accountable process of interpretation.[7]

The Role of the Researcher

I conducted this research both as an "insider" and an "outsider."[8] Like the participants, I was a woman engaged in Christian ministry and shared many of their faith perspectives and experiences. However, I did not share their experience, for example, where they were ministers in Protestant traditions or Catholic religious sisters; were Irish-born; nor in the variety of different ministries in which they served. I do not assume that all of the participants would see me as "inside" their immediate collegial group or ministerial experience.

5. "IPA researchers try to understand what an experience (object or an event) is like from the participant's perspective. Yet, at the same time, they try to formulate critical questions referring to the material." Pietkiewicz, and Smith, "Practical Guide," 363.

6. Swinton and Mowat state that "the choice of method and mode of analysis are deeply tied in with the epistemological positions which are assumed within the general outlook of the researcher and reflected in the research question." *Practical Theology*, 53. I would add that a philosophical coherence of method and topic opens up greater potential in the research.

7. This reflects an intentional hermeneutical methodology which shares the task of interpretation with stakeholders. For a discussion of hermeneutical theory in practical theology, see Brown, "Hermeneutical Theory," 112–22.

8. For a discussion on insider/outsider research, see Jarvis, *Practitioner-Researcher*.

Anonymity

All of the women ministering in Ireland are doing so as members of minorities in their particular traditions, and, in some cases, as members of small minorities. For this reason, if I were to name the specific denominations which are represented by participants this may compromise their anonymity. Although participants were very open and shared very personal aspects of their own stories, these had to be anonymised, and in some cases could not be shared. I have done my best to convey the content of what participants shared without compromising their anonymity.

Research Design Summary

The combination of these approaches and research design gave the research the following qualities:

- A philosophy which coheres with the aims of the research and the discipline of practical theology.[9]

- A grounding in qualitative research methods which serves the best outcome of the process.

- Research participants having primary importance in the project.

- Research participants having agency in determining the circumstances and content of their contribution, and the opportunity to review and corporately reflect on findings.

- Research results from women across the Christian denominations and the four corners of the island of Ireland.

Existing Research

There is no existing research on women in ministry in Ireland which investigates this experience across the churches.[10] Vocations Ireland commis-

9. It is an enquiry into human experience in the context of Christian ministry which leads to theological exploration and potential ecclesial reframing. It can be understood in terms of the tasks of practical theology proposed by Osmer: descriptive-empirical, interpretive, normative, pragmatic. Osmer, *Practical Theology*.

10. Relevant research from the Church of England includes Robbins and Greene's research with ordained women in the Church of England. Greene and Robbins, "Cost

sioned a report into religious vocations in Ireland for both female and male orders. This project did not set out to expose gender differences and did not ask questions about gender, however, the report has some interesting insights in the area of call which resonate with this study.[11]

THE WOMEN

I sent out the questionnaire on February 14, 2017. The first email response came back within five minutes and was a "woo hoo!" from a colleague. This was the first of a wave of positive responses which were to continue throughout the project. I believe that women participated because they wanted their stories to be heard.

The women who responded had been involved in ministry from four days to nearly sixty years. They were from the four largest church traditions on the island: Catholic, Church of Ireland, Methodist Church, and Presbyterian Church of Ireland, and from several other Christian denominations. A small minority were ministering in nondenominational settings. They were married, single, in relationships or in vows as members of religious congregations (sisters). Some were mothers, stepmothers and grandmothers, and they were ministering in all regions of Ireland.

The research findings present a cohort who spoke in terms of the privilege and joy of Christian ministry. Despite significant challenges, they expressed no regrets about their choice. They were sustained by prayer, Scripture, worship, family, and friends. A key finding was the importance of the sense of call in their lives and how this both motivated and sustained them in ministry. All acknowledged that within the other challenges of ministry their gender has played a part; that being a woman matters.

THIS BOOK

Part 1 will offer a brief background and context to the project, focussing on story of Christian ministry by women and current ecclesial contexts. Part 2 offers the findings from the research. Chapter 2 will present findings in the themes of call, theologies of ministry; inspiration and nourishment,

---

of a Calling"; Robbins and Greene, "Clergywomen's Experience of Ministry"; "Living Ministry Study," whose first report was issued in June 2017 and the large "Minding the Gap" report conducted by the Sophia Network.

11. Molina, "Religious Vocations in Ireland."

challenges and hopes. Chapter 3 will present further findings specifically in the areas of gender and denomination. Chapter 4 will offer some reflections on the discussions at the research gathering and how these contribute to further insights and questions for research.

Part 3 presents the individual interviews with women in chapter 5. Here I have interviewed Rev. Dr. Ruth Patterson, the first woman ordained in the Presbyterian Church and on the island of Ireland; Rev. Dr. Heather Morris, the first female president of the Methodist Church in Ireland; Sr. Margaret Kiely, a Sister of Mercy and founder of Tabor Group Addiction Services; Ms. Soline Humbert, a lifelong advocate for women's ordination in the Catholic Church, and the Most Reverend Patricia Storey, the first female bishop of the Church of Ireland.

PART I

1

The Background and Context of Women's Ministry in Ireland

WOMEN WHO MINISTER IN Ireland do so within a rich history which in-cludes first-century missionaries; saints and sisters; Roman prelates and Protestant pioneers. Here I offer a brief overview of some of the history and relevant factors, and some contemporary context for Christian women's ministries on the island of Ireland.

It is almost certain that the women of the fifth century would not have described themselves as "in ministry," as we might today, however, their life of prayer, evangelisation, and some service of the poor would contain the elements of modern understandings. Through the establishment of the apostolic congregations, and later growth in lay ministries in the Catho-lic tradition and the advent of missionary and ecclesial initiatives in the Church of Ireland and Protestant denominations, the presence of women's ministry is more surely discernible.[1]

---

1. Technically, professed women (sisters) are also "lay" but in general usage "lay" usu-ally means neither ordained nor religiously professed.

FEMALE RELIGIOUS ORDERS

Historically the ministry of women was seen in the work of professed religious women. The presence of religious sisters ensures that there have always been as many, if not more, women working in ministry on this island as men, challenging the impression that ministry is a minority or recent occupation for women.[2] Although the tradition of religious life is often associated with the Catholic tradition, the early part of this history belongs to women of all Christian denominations.

The first recorded women's monastery in Ireland was founded by Brigid in the fifth century in Kildare and this was soon followed by many others. Abbey life was focussed on prayer but also included education and service of the poor. The abbesses held considerable authority in the local churches. Hall notes that abbesses from the original Kildare foundation held particular influence as late as the twelfth century and quotes John Paparo, papal legate to Ireland in 1152.

> The abbesses of Kildare should no longer take precedence over the bishops in public assemblies.[3]

The foundations of convents peaked around 1150, and, following the Reformation, most of the abbeys were devastated under the dissolution laws of Henry VIII and into the seventeenth century under Elizabeth I. Following this and developments in religious life in Europe, new religious orders came to Ireland, including the Poor Clares in 1629; the Dominicans in 1643; the Carmelites and Augustinians in around 1651, and the Benedictines in 1687.

The Daughters of Charity, founded in France, represented a new development in women's religious life. Desiring to embrace a social ministry and to evade the strict rules regarding enclosure introduced in 1299, they did not adopt a constitution and took no solemn vows, thus freeing themselves for a charitable focus.[4] This opened the floodgates for unenclosed religious orders of women.

---

2. Peckham Magray notes that by 1901 women comprised 70 percent of the number of Catholic priests and nuns: *Transforming Power of the Nuns*, 9.

3. John Paparo, papal legate to Ireland in 1152, quoted in Hall, *Women and the Church*, 65.

4. This was the papal decretal *Periculoso*, 1299. A fuller history of the order can be found in O'Brien's *Leaving God for God*. The Daughters of Charity did not come to Ireland until 1855.

Two significant Irish additions came in the eighteenth and nineteenth centuries with Nano Nagle and her Presentation Order (1775) and Catherine McCauley and her Sisters of Mercy (1831). These focussed on care of the sick and poor, and education of women and girls.

Nano's Cork community became known as the Presentation Sisters. A song of the time recounted Nano's ministry:

> Lanes her hem touched were cured of hopelessness
> Her cloak was motherskirt that cuddled crowds,
> And desert tent for hearts loveparched and stray.
> Her lamp swung on a door to happiness.[5]

Catherine McAuley originally intended to found a group of "pious ladies" to serve the desperately needy people of Dublin, and founded an institution for homeless and distressed women which became known as the "House of Mercy." Her company, who visited homes, became known as the "walking nuns." Regan writes,

> By contagious, courageous concern for the spiritual and temporal welfare of the poor, the sick and the ignorant, she broke through the impossibilities of her time.[6]

The combination of prayer, work, and Christian vision gave women a way of being in ministry as a life commitment. Like the Mercy sisters, some orders were founded with philanthropic intent and founders did not originally intend founding religious congregations.[7]

The nineteenth and twentieth centuries saw huge growth in the religious orders and their influence. The number of women in religious life rose from 120 in 1800 to 1,500 in 1851. The post-independence census in 1926 recorded 9,564 female religious living in the twenty-six counties of the Free State. By the late 1960s the number increased to almost 15,500 on the island of Ireland.[8] It was estimated that a further 15,000 Irish sisters lived outside Ireland on the missions at that time.

---

5. Jerome Kiely, cited by Walsh, *Nano Nagle and the Presentation Sisters*, 88.

6. Regan, *Tender Courage*, 135.

7. Luddy quotes Catherine McAuley, who said, "I never intended founding a religious congregation. All I wanted was to serve the poor." *Women and Philanthropy*, 24.

8. Research and Development Unit of the Catholic Communications Institute of Ireland, "Survey of Catholic Clergy," 137–234; the Census of Ireland 1926–1991; and the Catholic Directory 1922–2004, cited in McKenna, *Made Holy*.

> For much of the twentieth century women religious formed
> the largest and most powerful group of professional women in
> Ireland.[9]

As well as the existing hospital and school foundations, sisters gradually became involved in social initiatives such as community projects, addiction treatment, and women's refuges. Many moved out of large convents and lived in smaller settings. Examples include the Good Shepherd work in Edel House Cork, founded by Sr. Colette Hickey (1972); Daughter of Mary and Joseph, Sr. Margaret Cusson's pastoral ministry in Dublin's Blackhall flats in the 1980s; and the Mercy Sisters' work in the area of addiction treatment opening *Aiseiri* (Sr. Eileen Fahey, 1983), *Tabor Lodge* (Sr. Margaret Kiely, 1989), *Hope House* (Sr. Attracta Canny and Sr. Dolores Duggan, 1993), and other treatment centres around the country. Margaret Kiely shares her story in part 3.

Recent developments have cast a shadow on the legacy of religious women. Investigations into care of children; Mother and Baby homes and Magdalen Laundries have found religious sisters to be guilty of neglect and abuses.[10] This evidence of historical wrongdoing by religious sisters is part of the context of their current ministry. Members are devastated by these revelations and how they have been received in Irish society. Molina describes the experience of trauma for religious women and men:

> Many religious members in Ireland are stepping in and out of
> hope and hopelessness and feel deeply hurt by media reports.[11]

Currently there are fifty-five women's congregations in Ireland.[12] The great majority of these women are over sixty years of age and there are very few candidates coming forward.[13] Congregations are now focussed on handing on their charism and mission to lay ministers, mostly women, some of whom participated in this study.

---

9. McKenna, *Made Holy*, 1.

10. Ryan, "Ryan Report," 2:6–16; McAleese, "Magdalen Laundries Report."

11. Molina, "Religious Vocations in Ireland," 10.

12. Information from the Association of Leaders and Missionaries of Ireland (AMRI).

13. AMRI does not have statistics for current numbers.

THE WIDER CATHOLIC CONTEXT

The effect of the Second Vatican Council (1962–65) on women and ministry in Ireland was twofold. The relaxation of rules for women in religious orders gave them freedom to pursue a greater variety of ministries which were reflective of their founding vision and charism.[14] There was a renewed theology of the laity which emphasised the role of lay people in many ministries in the church and on its behalf in wider society.[15] This led to a proliferation and flourishing of lay involvement and the development of training for lay ministers, mostly women. Many of the Catholic participants in this study came into ministry during these years.

Ordination

In 1987, in a meeting between Pope John Paul II and American Catholic clergy, Fr Frank McNulty requested that the Pope explore issues such as celibacy and the role of women. In response to the speech (submitted to the Vatican in advance) the Pope said: "I remember a song, 'It's a long way to Tipperary.'"[16]

While ministry is not synonymous with ordained ministry it is clearly a relevant factor. There is not room here for an exhaustive account of this issue but I will offer a brief overview of developments which most affect the context in which women minister in the Irish Catholic Church, including Tipperary!

There have been many women in history who have experienced a call to priesthood which has remained unfulfilled. Before her death St. Thérése of Lisieux said:

> God will take me at an age when I will not have had time to become a priest . . . I shall die before I have exercised my ministry.[17]

There has equally been a history of diverse voices claiming this ministry for women and asking the church to admit women to ordination. In 1970 Ludmila Javarova was ordained by Bishop Felix Davidek, who also

---

14. With the Vatican II document *Perfectae Caritatis*, religious congregations were to review their constitutions, initiating what O'Brien describes as a "whole-institution management-of-change process." *Leaving God for God*, 315.

15. For example, *Lumen Gentium* 12, and *Apostolicam Actuositatem* 10.

16. Hardy, "Only Hours after His Arrival."

17. Therese of Lisieux, *Journal of a Soul*, 119.

ordained a number of other women.[18] The Vatican did not deny that the ordinations had taken place but denied that women could undertake any priestly functions.

In 1976 the Vatican's commission of Scripture scholars were tasked to explore whether there was any evidence to preclude the ordination of women and they found none.

> It does not seem that the New Testament by itself alone will permit us to settle in a clear way and once and for all the problem of the possible accession of women to the presbyterate.[19]

The commission voted 12–15 in favour of the view that Scripture alone does not exclude the ordination of women, and 12–15 in favour of the view that the church could ordain women to the priesthood without going against Christ's original intentions. In the same year the Congregation for the Doctrine of the Faith's declaration *Inter Insigniores: On the Question of Admitting Women to the Ministerial Priesthood* confirmed the church's reservation of the ministerial priesthood to men.[20] This was followed in 1994 by Pope John Paul II's *Ordinatio Sacerdotalis*, which categorically reaffirmed this teaching. In 2016 Pope Francis confirmed this again, informally, speaking to journalists.[21]

Ireland: Brothers and Sisters in Christ

BASIC was founded in Ireland in 1993 by Soline Humbert, Colm Holmes, and Eamonn McCarthy to work and pray for the ordination of women to a renewed priesthood in the Catholic Church. Soline, whose full interview is in part 3, had experienced a call to priesthood as a teenager. The first BASIC conference took place in 1995 with speakers including Mary McAleese, who would become *Uachtarán na hÉireann*, and Enda McDonagh, who had been professor of moral theology in Maynooth for forty years.

---

18. John Wijngaards documents these in *The Ordination of Women*. After the end of Communist rule Javarova told her story in a book authored by Sister Miriam Therese Winter, *Out of the Depths*.

19. Report for the Pontifical Biblical Commission, 96, 92.

20. Congregation of the Doctrine of the Faith, *Inter Insigniores*.

21. 1994, http://w2.vatican.va/content/john-paul-ii/en/apost_letters/1994/documents/hf_jp-ii_apl_19940522_ordinatio-sacerdotalis.html and interviewed by the press https://www.ncronline.org/news/vatican/pope-francis-confirms-finality-ban-ordaining-women.

The 2001 conference, organised by an English Notre Dame sister, Myra Poole, and BASIC, was the first international conference of Women's Ordination Worldwide. Invited speakers included Aruna Gnanadson of the World Council of Churches, Joan Chittister, OSB, and John Wijngaards of the Housetop Centre in London. Extraordinary documents produced after the 2001 Women's Ordination Worldwide conference in Dublin included full texts from the presenters and an account of how attempts were made to "derail" the conference.[22] Vatican pressure on the World Council of Churches led to the withdrawal of Aruna Gnanadson; Sr. Myra Poole was threatened with expulsion from the Notre Dame congregation and pressure was also put on the leader of Joan Chittister's community in Erie. Prioress Christine Vladimiroff wrote back:

> I cannot be used by the Vatican to deliver an order of silencing. I did not see her participation in this conference as a "source of scandal" to the faithful as the Vatican alleges. I think the faithful can be scandalised when honest attempts to discuss questions of import to the Church are forbidden.[23]

BASIC merged with a sister organisation, We Are Church, in 2012 and continues its work to bring about the ordination of women.

Sarah MacDonald published an article in the *Irish Independent* on Holy Saturday 2018 in which she interviewed women about ministry. In it she quoted Mary McAleese's comments about women's ordination in the Catholic Church:

> I believe the theology on which [the ban on women's ordination] is based is pure codology. . . . Sooner or later, it'll fall apart, fall asunder under its own dead weight.[24]

THE DEVELOPMENT OF WOMEN'S MINISTRY IN THE CHURCH OF IRELAND AND PROTESTANT CHURCHES IN IRELAND

With the growth of Protestant churches in Ireland came expressions of women's ministry. Belfast Presbyterian Isabella Todd founded the North

---

22. McCarthy, *Now Is the Time.*
23. McCarthy, *Now Is the Time,* 83.
24. Mary McAleese, quoted by Sarah Macdonald, "Pure Codology," 3.

of Ireland Women's Suffrage Society in 1872 and Walsh notes the presence of Protestant female philanthropists in Dublin from the late nineteenth century.[25] Lady Arabella Denny was a Methodist who sought to convert young women and save them from prostitution. Two Methodist institutions run by women at this time were the Female Orphan Society and the Magdalen Society. Women were much more engaged in these expressions of Christian charity—now we would call them ministries—than in other places in Europe.

The Church of Ireland

Women in the Church of Ireland featured more prominently in ministry roles in the revival years of the nineteenth century and on into the twentieth. Acheson lists many women in Dublin who were involved in humanitarian work, funding projects, and religious encouragement.[26] They raised funds, met local needs, and both supported and embarked on foreign missions. Two English organisations also became established at this time: The Girls Friendly Society (1876) and the Mothers' Union (1887). Between 1874 and 1934 the Church Missionary Society sent 165 women overseas and Charlotte Pym of Monkstown founded the Leprosy Mission (1874).[27]

These roles were increasingly recognised and formalised. In 1892 the Deaconess and Missionary Training Institute was established in Dublin, and in 1902 a Women Workers' Settlement which prepared women to go and work in poor city parishes was opened in Belfast. Acheson quotes Archbishop Crozier, who said that women were

> the chief glory of our land. . . . They fill today the same office as Mary Magdalene on the morning of the Resurrection—they are *apostolae apostolorum*.[28]

In 1914, a petition to include women in parochial offices, signed by 1,400 women, was presented to the Church of Ireland and defeated. It was eventually passed in 1920, two years after women got the vote. In 1929 Lord Glenavy proposed the inclusion of women on Diocesan and General Synods, and, when defeated, set up the "Church of Ireland League," however,

---

25. Walsh, "Protestant Female Philanthropy."
26. Acheson, *History of the Church of Ireland*, 125–26.
27. Acheson, *History of the Church of Ireland*, 217.
28. Acheson, *History of the Church of Ireland*, 218 (no citation).

women were not admitted to these roles until 1949. In 1969 there were still only eighteen women on the General Synod but this was the year when the church elected to admit women to the office of reader which meant they could lead public prayer and preach. The first women, Daphne Wormwell, Patricia Hastings-Hardy, Audrey Smith, Thea Boyle, and Joan Rufli, were commissioned in this role in 1975.

In 1976 the General Synod of the Church of Ireland resolved that there was no theological objection to the ordination of women, but motions to remove the legal barriers to the ordination of women were not passed.[29] Eventually Synod passed a motion in favour of ordaining women to the diaconate in 1984, and women were finally admitted fully to orders in 1990. Kathleen Young and Irene Templeton were ordained in Belfast and, in the same year, Janet Caterall was ordained in Cork and Ginnie Kennerley in Dublin. Rev. Kennerley writes of her feelings during the opening procession:

> I was at once more and less than myself. I was the symbol of the fulfilment of so many hopes and struggles.[30]

In 2013 Rev. Pat Storey was selected for the diocese of Meath and Kildare and was ordained bishop on December 1 that year. She was the first female bishop in the Anglican Communion in Britain and Ireland. Pat shares her own story in part 3.

The Presbyterian Church in Ireland

Presbyterianism was introduced into Ireland through the Scottish settlers in Ulster but the church itself did not really become established until the later 1670s. The first women's organisation in the Presbyterian Church, the Zenana Mission, was founded in 1873 to send female teachers and medical workers, some of whom were doctors who, as women, could not work at home, to promote Christianity "among the women of the east." The first missionary to India was Susan Brown.

In the early twentieth century the Presbyterian Church saw women's ministry as a response to social problems brought about by industrialisation. The General Assembly made a recommendation for "an agency of fully

29. The context for this in the Anglican Communion is presented by Kennerley, *Embracing Women*, 12–20. She also acknowledges the influence of the ordination in the Presbyterian Church of Ruth Patterson.

30. Kennerley, *Embracing Women*, 107.

trained women workers," to be introduced in the local churches, resulting in the formation in 1905 of the Women's Association for Home Mission. Also in 1905, the Presbyterian Women's Union was formed for fellowship and to hear and discuss lectures on "edifying matters." This initiative was the foundation for the development in 1908 of the Deaconess Guild. Having been accepted via a rigorous application process, women paid for their own theological training. The first deaconess was Betty Barclay (1909) followed by Susan Watt and Mary Stevenson. Interestingly for participants of this study, in his sermon at her ordination, Rev. William Park stressed that because she was the first female deacon in Ireland people were looking up to her as an example.[31]

The ministry of deaconess comprised visitation with the poor and sick, and leading meetings. Their ordination also led members to ask for their admission to other roles traditionally held by men. In 1919 Rev. William McDowell called on the General Assembly to admit women to church courts and, in 1926, women were declared eligible for eldership and for membership of the church courts. In 1929 Revs. Strachan and MacMillan petitioned the General Assembly that women be admitted to the full ministry but this was defeated.[32]

Recently there has been a renewed interest in this ministry and Union Theological College has begun a course of training especially for women who wish to pursue this calling.[33] In 1973 the Presbyterian Church General Assembly, having considered relevant biblical texts, elected to ordain women to the full ministry, becoming the first Christian church in Ireland to do so.[34] The first woman ordained was Ruth Patterson. She tells her own story in part 3.

Presbyterian Women is now a lay association which is the modern amalgamation of previous women's groups. The aim of this group is specifically missional:

> . . . to provide an opportunity for women to have fellowship with
> one another and to seek to win women for Jesus Christ. It also

31. Holmes and McCracken, *Century of Service*, 10.

32. Holmes and McCracken, *Century of Service*, 20.

33. Union Theological College is the centre for theology and ministerial training for the Presbyterian Church and admits both women and men.

34. Baillie devotes some space to reactions to this which show the ambivalence present in the tradition even thirty-five years later: *Presbyterians in Ireland*, 179–86. This is also reflected in a letter to ministers written in 2008 by then moderator Donald J. Watts to clarify the church's position on women's ministry.

aims to encourage Christian discipleship and to foster support for local and global mission.[35]

The Methodist Church in Ireland

Women were involved in the revival of the eighteenth century and attracted to Methodism which allowed women to preach and to lead classes.[36] Cooney notes that there were Methodist women preaching during John Wesley's lifetime with his encouragement.[37] He documents the ministries of two Irish female preachers: Alice Cambridge of Bandon and Anne Lutton of County Down. Alice was regularly invited to speak at local gatherings. Faced with opposition she wrote to Wesley, who agreed: "I will not permit you to be silent when God commands you to speak."[38]

The death of Wesley in 1791 meant that women did not have this support. The 1802 conference resolved that it was

> contrary both to Scripture and to prudence that women should preach or should exhort in public.[39]

Alice was excluded from membership. Undeterred she preached at Methodist and also Presbyterian and Church of Ireland gatherings until her death in 1829. Anne Lutton preached, mostly at women's gatherings in Ireland and England, and men stood outside to hear her. Despite these examples, Hempton and Hill propose that women's preaching in Methodism should be seen as exceptional rather than accepted.[40]

By the middle of the nineteenth century, Methodism had become less "enthusiastic," and women were expected to speak only within their own circle. Methodist women were encouraged to pray and sew for the missions and engage in charitable works.[41] The conference of 1910 approved

---

35. Presbyterian Church in Ireland, "History of Presbyterian Women."

36. O'Dowd, *History of Women in Ireland*, 189.

37. Cooney, *Methodists in Ireland*, 121.

38. Hempton and Hill, "Women and Protestant Minorities," 202. Holmes notes that in a letter from 1787 Wesley gave full permission to Sarah Mallet to preach within a Methodist circuit. Holmes, *Religious Revivals*, 106.

39. Minutes of the Methodist conferences in Ireland, 1:52, cited in Hempton and Hill, *Women and Protestant Minorities* 202.

40. Hempton and Hill, *Women and Protestant Minorities*, 203.

41. Cooney describes the development of the Women's Department which fostered

of the admission of women to membership and the first, elected in 1911, were Miss P. Holmes, Mrs. Judge, and Mrs. S. T. Mercier. By the middle of the twentieth century there were several female local preachers and this number has increased steadily. The conferences of 1974 and 1975 resolved that women should be accepted to full ministry and the first woman, Ellen Whalley, was ordained in 1978. We shall see in part 3 that by the time the young Heather Morris received her call to ministry as a student it did not occur to her that her gender might be an obstacle. In June 2012 the Reverend Dr. Heather Morris was elected as the Methodist Church in Ireland's first female president. She took up her role in June 2013.

Quakers

Other Protestant congregations came to Ireland in the seventeenth century. These churches offered women a more equal role than the larger denominations though only Quakers supported women's preaching at that time. Fox wrote in 1656:

> May not the Spirit of Christ speak in the female as well in the male? Is he there to be limited?[42]

Kilroy names Anne Gould, Julianne Westwood, Elizabeth Smith, and Barbara Blagdon as early preachers.[43] The visit of George Fox to Dublin in 1669 encouraged women and Katherine McLoughlin preached publicly in the 1670s, and many others also, but they were often subjected to abuse.[44] By the end of the eighteenth century it had become unusual for women to preach beyond women's gatherings. Kilroy notes that they were edged out of influence and decision-making.[45]

The establishment of the Salvation Army in 1865 also opened preaching ministries to women. In 1880 four women under the command of Catherine Reynolds arrived in Belfast and within two years she and thirty-four

missionary interest and also contributed to the circuit at home. *Methodists in Ireland*, 123.

42. Fox, *Woman Learning in Silence*, 2, cited in Kilroy, "Women and the Reformation," 180.

43. Kilroy, "Women and the Reformation," 182. She recounts the tale of Blagdon being blamed for a storm at sea at sailors wanting to throw her overboard, and being threatened and accused of witchcraft.

44. O'Dowd, *History of Women in Ireland*, 175.

45. Kilroy, "Women and the Reformation," 189.

other women had established fifteen congregations (corps) across the north of Ireland. Holmes observes that the primary motivation of Protestant women at this time was their "call" to preach.[46]

The Moravian Church historically supported the strong participation of women and from the eighteenth century they occupied roles as deaconesses, eldresses, and, briefly, as presbyters (though there was then a gap 1790–1967). The Moravians have had a presence in Ireland since the middle of the eighteenth century.

Other Christian denominations are much newer to Ireland and have arrived with twentieth- and twenty-first-century immigration. The Orthodox churches and new Pentecostal churches are among the churches growing most quickly in Ireland.[47] In Orthodox churches women occupy roles including contributing with chanting during the service, undertaking managerial roles, and helping with the maintenance of the church. Traditionally, women also prepare the "prosphoro," bread that will be blessed during the Divine Liturgy to become the flesh of the Lord. Similarly, women by tradition prepare the "koliva," made for memorials.

The role of women in ministries in the Pentecostal churches varies across the expression of this tradition. In most churches, women are active in community and diaconal roles, and as leaders, but not as the main pastor.

This summary of this background of women's ministry tells us three things in particular. The first is that women will minister. Those who feel that God is calling them will do their utmost to answer the call, regardless of circumstances. Secondly, these women have needed resilience and perseverance in the face of opposition. Thirdly, the theological objections to the ministry of women have been and remain a formidable force and influence in Irish church traditions.

WOMEN'S MINISTRY IN CONTEMPORARY IRELAND

Christianity is deeply embedded in Ireland's history and culture, from the perception of the country as a "land of saints and scholars," to the sectarian troubles which have plagued relationships between Protestants and

---

46. Holmes, "Women Preachers," 89.

47. The development of the Orthodox churches is mapped by Kapalo, "Mediating Orthodoxy," 229–50. He proposes that it is legitimate to understand these churches together as a category (232).

Catholics. Although church attendance is falling across the island, the majority of Irish people claim a Christian identity.

Statistics are largely available where women occupy formal positions, particularly in ordained ministries. Where their ministries are less formal and not ordained these numbers tend not to be held centrally by the churches. In the Catholic Church this accounts for all of women's ministries and in other churches for a portion of them. There are approximately four hundred women ministering in Ireland as their main life choice. This includes women who are ordained as priests; deaconesses; women in parish, social, family, and youth ministries; diocesan advisors; and religious sisters. I base this estimate on the statistics received from the Christian churches and estimation of women in Catholic ministries by diocese.

The denominations operate on an all-Ireland basis and both the North and the Republic have been affected by sectarianism and a pattern of associating ecclesial belonging with political affiliation and cultural identity. Clearly this has been more strongly experienced in the North, where a diversity of Christian affiliations coupled with the Troubles has led to bloody conflict along Christian religious lines. Christianity in Ireland is never free of political nuance, and care is needed to acknowledge and respect differences and a painful past when working in ecumenical contexts.

WHY CONTROVERSIAL? THEOLOGICAL PERSPECTIVES ON WOMEN IN MINISTRY

All Christian traditions offer theological reasons for admission or non-admission of women to ministries. Because Jesus was not specific about all aspects of discipleship and church communities, interpretation has ensued and the place and role of women has been contested from the outset. These theologies and perspectives form a context for the ministry of women and this short summary will offer a context for the remarks of some participants about the theological milieu in which they minister.

Scripture

There is no doubt that the position and experience of women in ministry in Ireland has been influenced by the Scriptures. There are many fine presentations from theologians who explore this theme in detail.[48] Supporting women's ministry in particular are the gospel stories of the inclusive praxis of Jesus; the position of women as the first proclaimers of the resurrection; the depictions of women leaders active in the early church and key Pauline texts, particularly the baptismal code of Gal 3:28 which indicates that baptism "in Christ" means that the social divisions of nation, class and gender no longer apply.

Texts which are used by those opposed to women's ministry are the second creation story (Gen 2–3); the choice by Jesus of twelve male apostles, and the Pauline and post-Pauline texts in which the man is proposed as "head" of the woman, and that women should remain silent in the churches.[49] In the Catholic tradition, the maleness of Jesus and his choice of male apostles is a key argument, and in evangelical traditions the "headship" and silence passages are more influential.

The creation narrative of Gen 2–3, theologised as "the fall," is a key text in all Christian traditions and cultures. This event is seen as the catastrophe of the human story, in which the woman's infidelity leads to the loss of paradise. Because of this interpretation of the text, this story has become the metanarrative of the stereotyping of women as secondary, sinful, seductive, and blameworthy and Eve the symbol of the sinful seductress.[50]

Two important biblical characters also present in this debate are Mary, mother of Jesus, and Mary of Magdala. The biblical accounts of both provide a strong foundation for women's ministry. Mary, whose cooperation with God brought Christ into the world, and Mary, healed by Christ, leader of the female disciples and herald of the resurrection, exemplify discipleship, fidelity, strength, love, and mission. However, the subsequent interpretation and iconization of these figures has provided a counter to this influence. Mary, mother of Jesus, as the "new Eve," virgin and mother, and Mary of Magdala as a reformed prostitute in the mould of a repentant Eve have polarised expectations of women based on sexual behaviour and in relation to men.[51]

48. Here the classic text is Schüssler Fiorenza, *In Memory of Her*. She proposes that the praxis of Jesus is one of "inclusive wholeness," compatible with the Sophia tradition (132); sees the Twelve and the apostles as two separate groups and believes it likely that women were included as "apostles." "Apostleship of Women," 135.

49. For example, 1 Cor 11:2–16; 1 Cor 14:34; Eph 5:22–24; 1 Tim 2:11–15.

50. There are other interpretations, such as that found in Phyllis Trible, *God and the Rhetoric of Sexuality*.

51. Mary T. Malone notes that "neither image owed a great deal to their biblical forerunners." Malone, *Women and Christianity*, 2:254.

Schüssler Fiorenza recovers the stories of women who minister and lead in the early church.[52] She proposes that the women who are mentioned are the

> tip of the iceberg in which the most prominent women of the early Christian missionary movement surface, not as exceptions to the rule but as representatives of early Christian women who have survived androcentric redactions and historical silence. Their impact and importance must not be seen as exceptional, but must be understood within the structures of the early Christian missionary movement that allowed for the full participation and leadership of women.[53]

It is clear that women participated in the Pentecost event (Acts 2); hosted the "breaking of bread," in their homes and were coworkers with Paul.[54] The title of *diakonos* or deacon is used of women in the New Testament (see Rom 16 and 1 Tim 3) beginning a tradition of women's ministry which lasted until the eight century and has been renewed in the twentieth century.[55]

Most churches in Ireland, even where they are affiliated to international church identities, have the autonomy to espouse their own theologies and policies. Here I will briefly discuss the theological concepts and terms in the churches which most impact the ministry of women.

52. Schüssler Fiorenza, *In Memory of Her*, 160, 167.

53. Schüssler Fiorenza, *In Memory of Her*, 168.

54. Included here are Aphia (Phlm 2), Prisca (1 Cor 16; 19; Rom 16:5), and Nympha (Col 4:15). Paul describes women as coworker, teacher (Prisca, who with Aquila "risked their necks for my life," Rom 16:4), deacon, sister, benefactor (Phoebe, Rom 16:1) and apostle (Junia, Rom 16:7). Paul uses the same term *kopian* for his own teaching and the work of women, instructing the Thessalonians (5:12) and the Corinthians (1 Cor 16:1) to be subject to these coworkers and labourers. He commends Mary, Tryphaena, Tryphosa, and Persis for their "labour" in the Lord (Rom 16:6, 12). Euodia and Syntyche are singled out as coworkers and leaders (Phil 4:2–3). Other leaders are Chloe (1 Cor 1:11), a leader of the Corinthian church whose "people" write to Paul looking for guidance, and Lydia (Acts 16:14–15, 40).

55. An illuminating history is offered in Osiek et al., *Woman's Place*, or Zagano, *Women Deacons*.

The Church of Ireland and Protestant Churches

In many Christian traditions theologies of gender are proposed in terms of complementarianism and egalitarianism.[56] These views, while not entirely simple or exclusive, each claim biblical authority, drawing on the texts mentioned above.

Complementarianism

Complementarianism is the view that although women and men are equally valued by God, they are created different to one another, and their role and purpose in life is complementary. Men should be leaders, and women should be virtuous and loving within the family and church settings and should submit to the authority of men, particularly their husband or pastor. This is manifested in all areas of Christian living but especially in marriage and family and in church leadership. Typically, this view proposes the "spousal" nature of the woman and her calling to have such a relationship with Christ.[57]

Egalitarianism

Egalitarians propose that women and men are created equal and are called to ministry according to their gifts and calling, and not according to gender. This position may acknowledge differences between the sexes but does not accept that the results of these differences should be hierarchical or should privilege one over the other. This view is supported by those who support women's equality across the churches.

Egalitarianism is often posed as the opposite to complementarianism, however, as Stackhouse points out, these views are not necessarily mutually exclusive.[58] Where church members wish to remain faithful to a literal reading of the Bible but also wish to support women's leadership, this can

---

56. Elaine Storkey notes that this is particularly influenced by evangelicals in North America. "Gender and Evangelical Theology," 165. She exposes difficulties with the attempt to discover urge to find the true "characteristics of "biblical manhood and womanhood," and replicate these in our Christian communities today" (166).

57. Joyce, *Quiverfull*, 3.

58. Stackhouse, *Partners in Christ*, 15. Baillie notes that ministers are less likely to accept women's ministry than the people, and northern congregations are less likely to do so than those in the Republic. *Presbyterians in Ireland*, 218.

lead to a coexistence of perspectives and this will be borne out in the experiences of female ministers in part 2.

Ministries

DEACONESS AND DEACON

We have seen that this ministry was present in the very early church and it is now present in various Christian traditions. In the Presbyterian Church in Ireland it is entitled "deaconess," and reserved to women. The Church of Ireland ordains ministers as deacons "on the way" to priestly ordination but, unlike the Church of England, does not have a permanent diaconate.

In the Presbyterian Church in Ireland women are admitted to the presbyterate, the ministry, and the diaconate. The Book of the Constitution and Government of the PCI, also known as "the Code," lists definitions and roles for each. The ministry of elder is traced to earliest Christianity and exists in the category of teaching elder and ruling elder.

A deaconess has heard God's call and having been trained and commissioned exercises her ministry, which is

> complementary to the ministry of Word and Sacraments, in the spheres of pastoral counselling, education, social work, mission outreach, etc. She may also have some share in the leadership of worship.[59]

LAY MINISTRY

The taking up of service in the church and community is understood as lay ministry. This is seen as a biblical mandate and intrinsic to the life of a baptised person. In all of the traditions where there is a reduction in the number of people coming forward for ordained ministry there is a renewal of understanding and encouragement for lay ministries.

ORDAINED MINISTRY

In most Irish denominations, the priest, minister, presbyter is the person who presides at worship and liturgy; officiates at baptisms, Eucharist, or

59. Presbyterian Church in Ireland, "The Code," 303.

Holy Communion, and possibly other sacraments; preaches the gospel and exercises a ministry of pastoral care. He or she is seen as the official representative of the church; is paid for this role and takes this on as a lifetime choice accountable to a senior person or group such as a bishop or presbytery. This leadership role or ordination is open to women and men equally in the Presbyterian Church in Ireland; the Methodist Church in Ireland; the Church of Ireland; the Non-Subscribing Presbyterian Church; the Lutheran Church in Ireland; the Moravian Church; and the Salvation Army. In the Cherubim and Seraphim Church ordination is open to women and men but there are other gendered stipulations, such as the rule that women are not allowed in the holy of holies.

The member churches of the Association of Baptist Churches in Ireland do not accept women in ordained ministry but there are some female deacons in Irish Baptist churches. Rev. Karen Sethuraman is the minister of the Down Community and she was ordained as a Baptist minister by the Baptist Union of Great Britain.

Ordained ministry is reserved to men in the Free Presbyterian Church; the churches of the Congregational Union of Ireland; the Redeemed Christian Church of God; and the Plymouth Brethren Christian Church of the United Kingdom and Ireland.

The Catholic Church

Although expressions of Catholicism differ from place to place, policy decisions are taken on behalf of the global church in Rome.

Catholic teaching espouses a complementarian theology. A key text is John Paul II's *Mulieris Dignitatem*. This systematic presentation aims to study anthropological and theological factors in gender. John Paul states that Gen 2–3 expresses the truth about the creation of man and "especially woman."[60] Although in this document Pope John Paul names sexism as a sin and supports the dignity of women it is in Marian terms. He writes that equality must not lead to the "masculinisation" of women, whose nature is "spousal," and for whom motherhood is one vocation and the other is virginity.[61] John Paul II highlights the biblical evidence that only men were

---

60. John Paul II, *Mulieris Dignitatem*, 6.

61. John Paul II, *Mulieris Dignitatem*, 21.

chosen as apostles and were present at the Last Supper to indicate that only men can be ordained priests.[62]

Ordination

DEACON

In the Catholic Church the role of deacon is an ordained ministry reserved to men. Men are ordained to the transitional diaconate as part of the path to priesthood. Men are ordained as permanent deacons in a role which has always existed in the Catholic Church but which was only recently introduced by Irish dioceses.[63] Pope Francis has established the Study Commission on the Women's Diaconate (2 August 2016) to consider the church's position on admitting women to the diaconate. This group has so far failed to reach agreement.

THE CATHOLIC PRIESTHOOD

Catholic teaching proposes that because Jesus was a man, women cannot be ordained as priests. This is founded on a sacramental perspective with particular reference to the Eucharist. This view was reinforced by John Paul II in 1994 with *Ordinatio Sacerdotalis*. Here he states that Christ's choice of twelve men was a "free and sovereign act" and should not be interpreted as cultural conformity.[64] The Eucharist was instituted by Christ in explicit connection to the priestly service of the Twelve in which the priest acts *in persona Christi*, and must be male. He goes on:

> We declare that the Church has no faculty whatsoever to confer priestly ordination on women, and that this judgement is to be held definitively by all the faithful.[65]

Many counterarguments have been proposed for the ordination of women in the Catholic Church.[66] In the Irish context these are well-repre-

---

62. John Paul II, *Mulieris Dignitatem*, 26.

63. The first Irish permanent deacons were ordained in June 2012 in the Archdiocese of Dublin.

64. *Catechism of the Catholic Church* 1577.

65. John Paul II, Ordinatio Sacerdotalis, 4.

66. These are well-summarised on the website www.womenpriests.org.

sented by the documents which emerged from the BASIC 2001 international conference.[67] These contributions address the loss to the church of women's ministry; the lack of theological weight behind arguments against women; the limiting of God and the church in restricting ordained ministry to men; and the compelling nature of God's call in the lives of particular women.

It is not the purpose of this study to evaluate these arguments or their counterarguments. It is certainly possible to observe, however, that the 1996 statement banning further discussion of this topic did not make it go away.

LAY MINISTRY AND RELIGIOUS LIFE

As in the other traditions the lay Catholic is called to service by virtue of baptism. Since the Vatican Council there has been a burgeoning of lay ministries in the Catholic Church. As well as those who take on parish ministries of evangelisation, music, or social ministries in their locality in addition to their work and family life, there have been lay people, many of them women, who have moved into full-time professional ministerial roles. Many of the Catholic participants in this study have been doing this for years.

The Orthodox Churches

The Orthodox churches have a diaconal role which is reserved to men. This is currently under review. A 1988 Pan-Orthodox Consultation at Rhodes produced the document "The Place of Women in the Orthodox Church," which stated that the apostolic order of deaconesses should be revived. In 2016 the Patriarch of Alexandria appointed six nuns to be subdeaconesses within the church as a precursor to the reintroduction of women to the diaconate. It is possible that the other orthodox churches will follow. The Orthodox priesthood remains reserved to men for reasons very close to those of the Catholic Church.[68]

---

67. McCarthy, *Now Is the Time*, 65.

68. For an overview of the Orthodox position, please see Karkala-Zorba, "Ordination of Women."

Part I

Ecclesial Cultures

The experience of women in ministry is expressed in this research in the context of the history and theology of the churches they serve and there has been a cross fertilisation of ideology. For this reason, even where a church espouses an egalitarian theology, there may be experiences of inequality, and where there are restrictions on women some ministers can flourish within their own identity. Regional and political influences are also important, so generalisations rarely suffice. The real consequences of these theological positions in Irish churches will be seen in the testimonies of the women who minister here.

PART II

2

Findings (i)
Call and Ministry Life

THESE TWO CHAPTERS PRESENT, in the words of the women themselves, their experiences, concerns, and views as female ministers in the Christian churches. In the first of these chapters I will describe the ministries in which they are involved and the circumstances in which they work, and then present the findings in themes.

THE WORK

Women listed a wide range of work and contexts. Those in ordained or parish ministry included the leading of worship and sacraments, preaching, church leadership, administration, pastoral visitation, care for bereaved people, and other traditional roles. Many respondents described themselves as having an educational or teaching role; others worked in a particular area of ministry, such as liturgy, school or hospital chaplaincy, or spiritual accompaniment. Several were engaged in aspects of social justice, much of which was not directly in a church context. This included support for migrants, guiding a social justice project and addiction treatment. Some religious sisters were engaged in work for their congregations. Some participants worked in adult faith formation, evangelism and promotion of the Bible and others noted that ecumenical or interfaith activities were part of their work. Most of the work carried out by the women included an element of administration. Some mentioned that they were engaged in academic study while also carrying out their ministry. Others had an academic teaching role in addition to their ministry. Two indicated that they were involved in supporting the ministry of others through pastoral supervision.

Women were asked whether they were ordained; paid; had a formal contract and other benefits. These questions were asked in order to gain a sense of where women were finding their place and whether they felt satisfied with it. Some women were in ordained non-stipendiary ministry and therefore received no salary but some received expenses. Most others received remuneration for their work either through a formal contact or the terms of their ordained service. A minority, religious sisters and retired ministers, did not receive financial recompense for their work.

Some women in the Catholic Church were working in ministry on a verbal understanding with priests but expressed concern about what would happen if changes occurred. In these cases, clergy sometimes asked the women to undertake a variety of tasks which were not in their agreed role, such as administration and hospitality tasks. Others, also in the Catholic tradition, said they had been employed on a series of short-term contracts, which was unsatisfactory in terms of financial security and planning. Some Catholic women identified low pay and insecurity as an obstacle to their participation in ministry. Where these women had children, themselves few in number, they particularly expressed anxiety about being able to remain in ministry and meet their obligations as parents.

EMERGING THEMES

Here I have identified the prevalent themes in the questionnaire responses and the interviews. In this chapter I will consider the themes of call, theologies of ministry; inspiration and nourishment; challenges and hopes for the future.

1. Call: *"An Inward Impression on the Soul"*[1]

Although participants were not directly asked about call, this theme was the most consistent and prevalent among the responses. It arose mostly in

1. Wesley, "Sermon XI: The Witness of the Spirit."

response to questions about what drew women into ministry and what now sustains them during challenging times.

Most women described a key moment when they understood that they were being called by God to ministry. For many this was as part of a process of responding to God's call more generally and for some it was more an "out of the blue" experience. In many cases this was related to a sense of the meaning of their lives, expressed in phrases like "this is where I'm meant to be." For the great majority of the women this sense of call was the compelling and final word on their lives. It is notable that participants related these, sometimes extraordinary, experiences in simple and unvarnished ways, occasionally with humour.

For some this represented a change of direction. The plans they had made for themselves changed as a result of God's call.

> . . . while I had a permanent pensionable job in my day to day life—to actually do something more with my faith, and to help people more.

Sometimes this took place in personal prayer and sometimes when praying with others.

> We just prayed and something happened in the Lord. . . . I realised that whatever is going on God is certainly up to something. He's calling me to step out and go there. And I said "okay."

The call came unexpectedly for some:

> . . . and I remember just sitting up straight and going "this is it."

Some participants experienced call in the form of a startling physical sensation.

> I woke up with a voice calling my name and was shaken. Literally shoulder shaken, nobody there, and I got up and walked to the sanctuary . . . and I turned around and realised where I was meant to be.
>
> They said "it's time to pray with N," and the pain switched off just like that. So that was the Lord saying, "That's the way you go." I said, "That's the way I go."

Some women disclosed their call to discover that other people had already understood that they were called to ministry:

They gathered round and they could see on my face and I said, "I'm meant to be a priest." "O glory be," they said, "we thought we were going to have to tell you."

I told my husband what I was going to do before I went down to the rector and he said to me, "I've been waiting for a year for you to say this."

As well as these experiences women spoke about the call to ministry as suiting their nature and experience. It was a process of discernment which acknowledged their existing preferences and direction in life. Through questioning and testing they eventually became sure of their calling:

I loved leading prayer, I loved being with people, and it just made sense.

I always felt I was called to be a sister. Since I was quite small. I don't remember when it started but I always knew that's what God wanted.

I prayed a lot about it, from the glimmering, it's like when you have a thought and everything kind of coalesces on it. It was like every hymn was speaking directly to me and every Bible reading it was all "who shall I call?" It was everything seemed to be hammering home: "yes thicko it is you I'm calling! Off you go."

A singular and often remarkable aspect of being called and a continuing sense of vocation was how strong and compelling it was. Women felt "pursued," and "had no peace," until they responded. Sometimes they heard themselves say things which they hadn't planned to say or had even thought beforehand.

I looked up at her, and I hadn't premeditated these words and I said, "I think God wants me to be a nun." And as soon as I'd said it I wanted my tongue cut out . . . inside my heart was pounding and it wouldn't go away all that evening so I bargained with God. I said look I'll look this up but I don't know what it means. But anyway to make a long story short for the three years I did my training, every single day it was with me. I could not get away from it.

And I heard myself say to my boss one day, "Well if I have to choose between studying theology and this job I know what my choice is going to be." I was trying not to show it on my face but I was thinking, "Who said that?"

A prevalent image in this respect was that of doors opening. This image was used by participants both in terms of their overall calling and also as a way of testing whether it was "right" for them to pursue it. If the doors opened they could feel more certain that God was behind their decision.

> If it's not meant to be then the doors won't open but if it is meant to be then they will. . . . I just knew that the doors would open. And it would just happen.

> So I just think God has worked my life with all these little kind of doors without me even trying.

> Then I turned and walked back. . . . The college is locked during the holiday and if the door is closed you might have to ring a buzzer and I would have turned and walked away. But it so happened that someone was coming out and held the door open for me. And I went in.

For some respondents the call to ministry came with their conversion to Christian faith, or a deepening of an existing faith.

> I was led to make the decision about surrendering my life to God, as in letting go of my driving the wheel, even though I thought God was doing it but actually it was me driving a lot of it. And letting go in a very, very deep way.

> I came into the church and I had the most remarkable sensation of homecoming. That's the only way I can describe it. It was as if this place had been waiting for me all my life and I had somehow not known it.

For many participants the call was the sustaining factor that would keep them going in times of challenge. Even when times became difficult or when other people challenged their participation in ministry, even when there appeared to be no place for them, their sense of God's abiding call meant that they continued against the odds.

> The light wouldn't go out. . . . I could feel I was called to ordination and it wouldn't go away.

> The sense of knowing that this is what God requires of me and being peaceful with that despite the levels of difficulty even angry disappointment that there are in the church and the sense in which so many felt let down.

Sometimes I think a different answer would be less traumatic, less painful, but, it's, you can't make up truth, do you know what I mean? So sometimes I wouldn't mind if I could find a different answer but I can't and I can't make something else be this. So therefore, I'm stuck with it or it's stuck with me. A lot of the time just a sense of, yes maybe you know this is the only way I can live this life, no matter how many other ways I'd prefer to live it.

While called to ministry some women felt that a particular role was indicated. They felt attracted to parish ministry or the missions; pastoral care, youth, or preaching. Some resisted pressure to move into alternative areas of ministry, and others found themselves in ministries to which they did not feel especially suited.

A kind of feeling that I should be doing something about social things really . . . and I realised that what I was being drawn to wasn't social work it was actually ministry.

I never felt drawn to lay ministry. I liked and wanted the sacramental side.

It was definitely parish ministry. Earlier on in my career . . . the bishop tried to push me into chaplaincy and I resisted. . . . I like the variety and the diversity of parish work.

When I first encountered God the sense was "God I want to tell others about this!" . . . It was the sense of excitement and joy of—I hadn't heard this before this. And now I have heard God's good news and so I want to tell others.

Some women spoke with hindsight and humour about how they see this call now:

My faith and the belief that I'm doing what I've been called to do and I was called to do it therefore it, you know, it's my duty, my privilege to do it.

You always think you're going to change the world. You always think you're going to be the saviour of the church, you're going to be the greatest pastor, the greatest evangelist, the greatest Bible teacher!

But it's that journey of all the time you're coming with this huge vision and then you see the reality. But I want it to be more than the "reality." I don't just want a civil service job in the church.

I thought that someone would take me aside and say to me that
this is not actually the path for you, think of something else. And
so at all stages going through I have expected someone to say,
"Get a grip."

The influence of other people: family, friends, and faith community
played an important role in the call of women even when there was some
doubt about their formal role in their church. Many women had an initial
sense of self-doubt and a need to test the call. When it was affirmed by others this was always seen as a confirmation that God had indeed made this
call. Even in this latter case the fact that no one told this minister to "get a
grip" meant that she felt emboldened to continue along the path to ministry!

2. Purpose and Theology of Ministry: *"Drawn into Fullness of Life"*

Women were not specifically asked about their theology of ministry but
many spoke of how they understood their role. This came across in reflecting on their story, how they express meaning in their lives and in
what they do.

Many participants understood ministry essentially as doing God's
work: that they are called to participate in this and that they will be empowered so to do. There is very little evidence of ego in this theology and it
indicates an accompanying spirituality of trust and abandonment.

Because it's the kingdom. It's the upside-down kingdom. It has to
be my faith in God. And God does this because it's not me.

I suppose that all of us, all Christians together and no matter
what denomination we're in could better reflect the life of Jesus
Christ. And that his acceptance and his inclusion of people that
were marginalised and his peace and his grace; that we could
reflect that better.

Some respondents emphasised the sharing of the gospel message or
God's love as central to ministry. They wanted to encourage others to have
a relationship with Jesus.

I had a passion to bring other people to Christ and to have that
personal relationship with him.

Being a translator from my experience of divine love into lan-
guages that connect with peoples' experiences. Being part of moments where together we can create a context/space where we can

experience the Divine at work and loving us. It's about awareness
and awakening to Presence.

I also feel that I'm helping to hand on the faith, to keep the faith
alive and to help hand it on again.

Pastoral care was a key theme in the understanding of ministry. Participants highlighted their role in being "there" for people, particularly those experiencing troubles.

It would have been to be in places where people had nothing and
to be with them and to bring about a good quality of life.

Anybody who wants to find me knows where I am. So I think
that's just the ministry of being, just to be there.

It's a great privilege to be with people who are dying, and people
who are very ill, and who ask for you to be there.

Respondents acknowledge that their experience of ministry has brought spiritual growth and development.

And I'm just so glad that God gave me all those experiences including the hard ones and the grief, that enabled me to be who I
am today in ministry.

I think all of us are called into mysticism. . . . You know that's all
our story but it's being able to be aware of it to be highlighted.

But I could just talk to Jesus like he's sitting there and I'd be giving
out and . . . sometimes I don't think I'm doing the right thing, but
it's peaceful so I feel like there's that gift of assurance, yes.

[Ministry] pushes me in a good way to develop my relationship
with the Lord, makes me more attentive to my prayer life.

There has been some movement among the women between denominations; from religious life (sisters) to lay life and from lay ministry to ordained ministry. This may raise a question of whether women move more freely or frequently within church or ministerial belonging than men. This is what some said about their vocation in terms of being ordained or not.

I'd have a big thing about the distinction between vocation and
ministry, that the vocation is our whole self, who am I called to be,
and particularly in our ministries. The particular ministry is for
a particular time you're in a particular role in a particular place.

I guess the only thing that has changed is that I usually if I'm out and about I wear a collar and therefore you're recognised as what you and there has been a few occasions where complete strangers have stopped me, be it in the hospital or on the street or whatever, and said, especially in the hospital, "Oh can you come quickly . . . I have somebody in intensive care" or whatever.

But I don't need the permission of ordination whatever about the grace of it.

There was a recurring theme that women wanted to be "alongside" the people they served and variations of the phrase "get stuck in" were used a total of seven times. This was exemplified by this minister:

I actually like getting out and cutting the grass on a sit-on lawn mower. It clears my head . . . and parishioners see me over the fence and they'll wave and I'll stop with them. I could do half a dozen visits by cutting the grass, you know?

And when it comes to doing things around the parish I roll my sleeves up and I get stuck in. . . . They know that I will literally get on my hands and knees and scrub something if they're scrubbing something. . . . Because my theory is that I wouldn't ask anyone else to do stuff that I wasn't prepared to do myself. And just because I'm a woman doesn't make it any different.

It is also important to women in ministry that they know their limitations, ask for help, and take time out.

If there's something [physical] I can't do I'll say, "Look for goodness' sake would yous come over here and carry this? What do you think I am some sort of big hefty man?" So I know my limitations and I know what I can and can't do and I think that people, especially here, they respect that.

I've seen a number of ministries ruined by people not being open with their congregations about what the issues are and the problems.

Sometimes you just need to take time and not feel guilty and I'm learning. I'm learning to say "no."

But I had to have some boundaries. . . . It's not fair to them [her children]. . . . It's not their ministry. I'm their mammy. That has been the hardest I think.

Women identified the centrality of team and community to their understanding of ministry throughout. None of the respondents said that they preferred to work alone and many mentioned the importance of community, collaboration, and shared decision-making. For some of those who lived with others in couples, families or religious communities this element was described as integral to their theology of ministry.

> There's a few dynamics. One is that I have chosen to live my life within the [religious congregation] and from that base I go out to ministry. . . . It's the life of somebody living in community.

> I think particularly for us [mentions a church], the idea of community is really important. . . . I don't think you can be out on a limb, and I'll serve you but you can't serve me. You know I think there has to be mutuality. And I don't like the idea of being six feet above contradiction. It's collaborative.

> Actually, our understanding is Trinitarian. It's relationship. It's community. If that's our model of priesthood. . . . When I talk about women in ministry I want to talk out of that, that relationality.

The social dimension of ministry was emphasised: to be at parties or drama groups; to mix and to encourage a community dimension in faith communities.

> . . . and that has been my kind of goal as well—to create community. I wanted to show people how you can be connected to church without being a holy Joe.

> I was at a birthday party on Sunday. I didn't know anybody at it, but it was just the kind of hanging round and listening and chatting and just giving the time. Well Jesus spent a lot of time hanging around.

Some women identified a liminality to their ministry for a variety of reasons. The element of a ministry in the gaps, or on the margins came across. Several felt it inevitable that female ministers would not find themselves at the centre because of the contested nature of women's ministry and because it was normatively male.

> It seems to be part of my life because [place in Northern Ireland] is a fault line. . . . And then fault lines in the church as well. Between men and women and between what's expected. . . . I have to . . . try and do ministry in the gaps.

> I've never been the right person in terms of the Institution, but I have still been in ministry my whole life. I'm the right person for God's people. It has meant that I have never had a permanent pensionable job. It has meant real poverty and I would never admit that but I think that's where the Spirit is, in all our poverty. I'll never fit but maybe if I fitted and got comfortable I wouldn't reach people. God is at the margins. As a woman I will never be anything but marginal.

Interestingly, when asked about their work, in addition to describing their activities and responsibilities, some participants used words such as disciple, witness, animator, encourager, and facilitator. These words are less descriptive of the activities undertaken but echo New Testament themes. This theological language coheres with an understanding of ministry which is not defined only by a particular activity and which aligns itself with the call and work of God.

Related to this, and finally, it was clear for many of the women that their theology of ministry was closely related to their sense of self; their authenticity and personal identity.

> That's who I am. I'm happiest when I'm with people.

> I don't think there's any way a woman would survive in ministry if she hadn't done a lot of personal work in terms of recognising her own strength and integrity and desire for goodness and for good things to happen for people and for life to be meaningful. I think you have to have . . . experienced losses, failures, relationships, and then to be able to stand on your own two feet and know that even though you're being rebuffed that what you're standing for is true; it's just; it's fair and it's of God.

> My best friend turning around and saying, "No one is going to want to take you on because you're so . . . no one will take you on with those views." And I said, "If they don't they don't. This is who I am and I believe that God called me for who I am. Not for some watered-down version of myself."

> I have no regrets, I do what I am, but it has been very costly.

3. What Sustains, Nourishes, Inspires? "*Not My Faith but God's Presence*"

Here women wrote and talked about the nourishing, supportive, and inspirational elements in their lives and ministries. The most common theme in this category was that of prayer and spirituality. The spiritual practice of these ministers was the most sustaining factor of their ministries. Every person identified this element.

> Prayer really. And relying an awful lot on . . . I always feel that I walk in step with Jesus. . . . That he's there with me all the time.

> I suppose that is what sustains me really, that I have absolute love for the Eucharist and love for my faith.

> My faith and the belief that I'm doing what I've been called to do. . . . Jesus didn't find it easy, it was difficult for him. And he's my example and although I sometimes you know forget to look at him or to think deeply enough, you know, I believe that he's there with me and he will sustain me.

Participants also strongly included their family and friends; their faith communities and colleagues when speaking of what sustains and inspires them. They saw their ministry as functioning within a personal and ecclesial community.

> I do have the support of my lovely community [of religious sisters].

> I feel free with the clergy that I know, that I work with, who are available to me, either for the work or personally if I have—I'm a person too; a human being that sometimes has problems.

> My colleagues who are a good example; who pray with me; who listen to me moaning and groaning! Most of these are [male] priests and my ministry would be impossible without them because they keep inviting me in.

> My family life, the congregation . . . let your congregations know you and love you and care for you.

> Astounding and unstinting support from my husband.

> My husband. Through training and ministry . . . so there were times where I was on the phone and I'd say, "I'm coming home." And my husband said, "That's okay, yes come on home because

you'll be on the first plane back again." . . . He could obviously see the bigger picture.

Many women have regular supervision or spiritual direction, though two women report that they would like it but can't afford it. Participants welcome the sense of accountability, challenge, and support where this is possible.

I would have one or two people who I would be able to say it to, to be a bit objective—am I reading this right? Or was I a bit unreasonable?

Then I need to mind myself within all of that as well, while making sure that I have regular contact with my spiritual director and that that relationship is maintained to a level that I'm happy with, that I know I'm being supported from sides.

Some respondents highlighted areas of their ministry which they found nourishing and inspiring.

Praying with people. That actually all the rest I can question . . . but actually when it's just about hard core praying I kind of think, "Well yes." I've no question about that.

Getting a sense from somebody that they accessed a little glimpse of God being a caring, loving, joyous, delighting-in God, as op-posed to "but I should love God shouldn't I?"

I think that what sustains me in ministry is my congregation and moments like today [she had visited a family in the hospice] where you feel you can . . . go in to someone and they just say something like, "That's what he needed." I can do that.

Empowering people. That's really God's work.

Women identified those who had been role models or had been espe-cially inspirational. They were inspired by personal qualities such as holi-ness and wisdom, and by their ministry and service of others. They mostly did not highlight gender in this area and where gender was mentioned it was specifically in the area of example of being a woman in ministry.

But I had a wonderful rector [N] who was extremely grounded and very spiritual. He was a wonderful role model. He was what I wanted to be.

N was the first bishop I worked for where I went I absolutely trust and believe in this man.

I have a lot of faith in St. Teresa . . . because I like her mind set. You know she wanted to become a priest. And I like that she was ferocious in her love for Jesus. I really like that ferocity.

I am looking to female ministers in other denominations who assume their role so naturally.

The experience of training and formation was something which women took with them as nourishment to their ministry long after it was over. They valued all opportunities for further formation and regretted where these were not available or were prohibitively expensive.

I got involved in so many things in the college, in the faith community; in the college itself, that has given me the skills that are worth more than that piece of paper.

He offered me a place in [formation centre] and I went there for about six weeks. That saved my life.

4. Hopes for the Future: *"To Follow Jesus Faithfully"*

Respondents generally did not express hopes for the future unless specifically asked. When asked this was a general question about "hopes for the future" which could have been answered in terms of personal aspirations or in any other sense.

Where participants answered personally they expressed no ambitions for promotion or career development, even when the contexts of their ministries provided for this. Their responses were couched in terms of vocation and service.

That I will never let my Lord down, and that I will be given the strength to continue working despite the changes in my life which are coming.

That I continue to follow Jesus faithfully and this keeps my ministry relevant and fresh.

Hope to grow myself in all these ways—that I am kept faithful and given godly passion to do what I do—that I live and minister in a way that honours Jesus my Saviour and his spirit within me. To get better at preaching!

Where participants presented hopes other than personal concerns they focussed on their church communities and concerns for their wider denomination. Some of these focussed on social development:

> So my aspirations I suppose would be to see the congregation grow; to see social bonds develop with people.

On faith and church:

> I'd like to see people being ready to discuss the Bible, not afraid to exchange ideas; not afraid of the fact that they take different positions or interpret things differently.

> [Regarding retreat work:] I'd love to be able to do something like that at parish level, because it's only in the experiential that things will change.

> That Spiritual Accompaniment may be recognised as a valid and important ministry within the church. That supportive faith sharing structures would be nourished, and adequately formed laity be supported in shaping the future of a more lay centred Christian community.

Some respondents expressed personal hopes in the area of ministry:

> That's [prison chaplaincy] where I would wish to be if I had the choice.

> Well I'm now [into elder years]. I'm as busy as ever. I'm not going to last forever. I have to sort of see how I can pass on the baton when it's right.

> I've got [n] years to go. My hopes would still be the same. To be the best preacher I can, to be the best pastor I can; to be the best evangelist I can.

> Although the see house is very nice. I was going to go and measure some curtains there! No I have never had any desire or anything to climb any ladder. I'm just happy to be what I am.

> My hopes for myself: not to mess up too much; not to let people down. To do the best that I can.

Many expressed a hope and desire for support, formation, and nourishment for women in ministry.

> And I do think too that there should be some support group or some way of meeting with other people in ministry. I don't care

what church, denomination or anything, just to share kind of experience of women—I mean that's how you learn; that's how you
grow, meeting other people and communicating with them.

I think I would like to grow or reflect on how one might grow a
solidarity among women ministers.

Concerns about the future, fears.

These concerns arose when participants were asked about their hopes.
They acknowledged the question but used the opportunity to express
concerns.

God Anne. I'm beginning to wonder do I have any hopes for future. My worry, and I know you're asking me for a hope, so my
hope would be that we could explore and create ministerial opportunities for women and men as opposed to clergy, which meet
the pastoral needs of people . . . as a place that gives them access
to the transcendent; to meaning in life. I think we will say, "Well
there's this little opening, so can we envisage something in that
box," rather than saying, "Actually how do we share the good news
of Christ at this time, in this place in a way that people can access?"

And that somebody won't come in and blanketly decide that we're
not needed any more and that is my biggest fear.

I will say this for this interview. I am going to leave. I am leaving.
So that is the sadness. I have worked through ministry and I won't
now continue because this is not ministry as I understand it. This
is trying to follow a male model . . . where I'm not considered good
enough.

5. The Experience of the Research Process

I did not solicit comments about the research itself but many women, both
in questionnaires and the interviews, made reference to their participation
in the research process. Many expressed appreciation on the grounds that
someone was hearing and documenting their experience.

Thank you for giving us this forum.

I think the fact that you are doing this project is a clear and a useful
directional statement and it will be very interesting to see what
comes from that. . . . It's always very useful to have some concrete
piece of research that can form a basis for discussion, can stimulate

thought, and can be all the things that that kind of document or report can be.

You don't want to be a complainer as it will get you nowhere. But these things should be addressed and what you're doing will help that to happen.

A significant minority of participants expressed concerns about anonymity. At various stages in interviews women expressed concern about what they were saying, often in a good-humoured way:

You'd better not put that in!

Strike that bit!

One woman who had agreed to be interviewed demurred on the day because of her concern that she might be identified, despite assurances to the contrary. One woman expressed her concern that my own ministry might be adversely affected by my association with this research. There was in places a sense of nervousness about how participation might be seen by male leaders. This in itself could be seen as an indication that women feel somewhat insecure in their ministry roles and contexts and that appeasing men is still perceived as a necessary part of their reality.

This chapter has been very much about the women in their own terms. Chapter 4 will explore what the women have said about gender and denomination.

3

Findings (ii)
Gender and Denomination

IN THIS CHAPTER I will focus on the two remaining themes of gender and denomination. Because of the title and aims of the research, all of the responses are in some way gendered. There is therefore considerable overlap between this and other categories. However, some women did identify particular issues which arose in their ministry and churches because they were women. Where they have done so I have considered these first. Where the gendered experience was due to particular denominational rules or issues I have presented this in the denominational context.

6. Gender: *"Because I Am a Woman . . ."*

Participants noted that there were many areas which were the same for women and men. A recurring observation in the project was that all ministers experience their role differently and it is not always clear where gender is the sole factor. I will begin with a summary of comments about difference and then take general themes emerging from the data as a whole.

(i) Is the Experience of Ministry Different for Women?

When asked, "Do you think your experience of ministry is different to that of male colleagues?" sixteen (of twenty-two) questionnaire respondents said "yes." Others said "no" or "not substantially," but each of these qualified their answer giving some examples of difference but explaining that this was not significant. Overall, women feel that their experience of ministry is different to that of their male colleagues.

Where respondents said "yes," and even when they said "no," they indicated a variety of contexts and reasons for the differences they experienced. These can be summarised in the areas of home; ministerial context; church structures and others.

HOME

The data revealed home life to be particularly affected by gender. Housework and childcare responsibilities fell to the woman, who usually maintained traditional domestic roles as well as her ministerial responsibilities. Balancing work and family demands was a constant challenge for participants with children.

The question of the partner of a female minister is also an area of difference. The clergy wife has a particular role and status in many denominations and the clergy husband does not. Ordained participants said that they sometimes felt expected to fulfil the roles of minister and minister's wife. Others said that their husbands were excluded because there was no traditional role for them. Where both partners were ministers an issue arose where arrangements for both ministries were not in place and one partner would take a lesser role or travel to accommodate the other, placing a strain on the relationship. There were no examples of couples in ministry working as a team though one participant mentioned this being the case with a Salvation Army couple she knew. Married Catholic ministers said that their husbands were mostly ignored, and excluded on occasions like Christmas meals or liturgical celebrations. One noted that her ministry depended on her husband being at home to look after the children at evenings and weekends so she could fulfil her role and this commitment was never acknowledged by her single colleagues. One Catholic minister with children felt that her children were seen as a nuisance with their collection times, school holidays and dentist visits, and another said that her clergy colleagues were careful to accommodate her role as a parent and constantly reassured her that family came first.

MINISTERIAL CONTEXT

In this area the majority of questionnaire respondents and interviewees noted a gender difference. They indicated that the male is perceived as the norm and women are the exceptions or newcomers. Men's work is more valued and they are invited into more interesting and formal roles, more leadership and work with greater budgets and responsibility. Women can be confined to certain ministries, particularly with children or families. Some participants felt this may be unconscious bias rather than deliberate discrimination.

Many women observed a difference with regard to how they were perceived. In Catholic contexts they noted that some people "did not know what to do with them," because they were not the priest. The priestly role had been so completely all-encompassing in Ireland that people could not imagine a complementary ministerial role occupied by a woman. This was sometimes mitigated if they were a religious sister, but here a sister made the observation that the parish was seen entirely as the domain of the priest. When she worked in a hospital or school owned by her order she had influence, but when she moved to a parish setting she had no influence and was seen as occupying a position very much inferior to the priest. Clearly this issue is related to a clerical mentality but the fact that the ordination was a male preserve necessarily genders this situation. The difference between the parish or diocesan contexts will be of interest when considering the Catholic context in the next section.

Where women were ordained they noted that often they were seen not simply as a priest but as a "woman priest," and therefore perceived as having less authority despite being as qualified as male ordained colleagues. One woman felt that there were lower expectations of her because she was a woman, another that she was there for family and music ministries, "not theology, not money and not decisions." Several women said that when women occupied positions traditionally held by men this changed perceptions and expectations and was the most effective means of opening the way to other women.

CHURCH STRUCTURES

Several women observed that while structures are necessary, the structures in church are power structures, there to maintain certain hierarchies of values, and women rarely, if ever, benefit from these. This hierarchy has been designed by and for men and will value and promote men. Examples of this are that women are less likely to get a job in a theological college or as a bishop. Catholic women find they have no title or that their title contains the words "assistant," or "worker," rather than "director," or "executive." These women also noted that in a culture which makes much of anniversaries of priesthood, their anniversaries or number of years in ministry are disregarded. They say they are always seen as extra, amateur, or temporary and have no place at all in church structures. This makes it easy for the church to treat them poorly and even discard them. Many of these women noted that they were more qualified and experienced than many of the male colleagues who had power or oversight over their ministries.

In church structures women said they feel as though there are seen as a threat to the norm, and there to be controlled. Men, however, are expected to take charge, and are seen as reliable and qualified, whether or not this is the case. Where women have non-stipendiary roles, they have less status. One noted that while it was acknowledged that she had had a full professional career before entering non-stipendiary ministry, with many transferrable skills, she still felt that she was expected to "stay in her place," when with full-time paid ministers. There was no contribution which viewed church structures in any denomination as beneficial or supportive to women and women's ministries.

OTHER

Another area of difference is that women are seen to represent other women. Where women have offended this is seen as being typical of all women. Several participants felt that it is expected that they have to prove themselves and explain themselves constantly, even after showing their worth in multiple ways. It is difficult for a woman to do an ordinary job. She is expected to be extraordinary to show that women can succeed in ministry. One person pointed out that even if she ministered for ten years without comment, if she were to comment on fairness for women she would be labelled as a feminist and a troublemaker and her previous record would show that even the women who seemed trustworthy were "secretly antiestablishment."

Some women reported feeling isolated. Catholic women expressed the sense of having no colleagues because they are in individual roles. Where they might see priests as colleagues, priests do not treat them as colleagues. This is also a problem in denominations where women are ordained. They are often the sole woman in an area and they can find themselves excluded from clergy events which can still be "boys' clubs."

(ii) Discrimination: Intentional and Unintentional

Some women spoke about their experience of direct misogyny or discrimination. This was experienced by a minority of women as they applied for ordination, promotion, or particular ministries. It was also present in actions, attitudes, and comments which they felt would not have been applied to men in the same circumstances. For some women this was a general sense of hostility; for one person it was a sense of physical threat; others had experienced sexual harassment and for others it was the expectation that they would play a domestic role in the parish such as making jam for the parish fete.

Participants drew a distinction between this experience in the context of employment or structure and a difference in attitude to male and female ministers which they experienced from congregation members. Some congregation members moved to other churches or asked other clergy to conduct weddings or funerals because the new minister was female. Other women felt that people respected them less or refused to acknowledge their authority in situations where traditionally the minister would be deferred to.

> I've had people refuse to let me bury their relatives.

> There was one instance where some young men were of the opinion that they knew better than I did and simply would not cooperate and challenged me a lot. And that was difficult.

Women accept that gendered theology influences how they are seen in their traditions but also wonder whether this may also cover a simple prejudice. Some women feel that there is a hatred of women present in churches others name this as fear and a wish to control.

> I'm not sure that the same men would be terribly happy with women in other—say politics or other public roles. So, I think that if I were to tell you my personal opinion which would be my own prejudice and bias . . . it would be that they are chauvinistic anyway and that their interpretation of St. Paul supports their chauvinism but who knows? I could be utterly misjudging them. I don't think I am but!

I think it's not hate, but fear. The Catholic hierarchy is frightened of women. They feel they can't control us and that's what they're about—control. They would do anything to get rid of us. Maybe the fear turns into hate after a while. . . . Yes, I think I have felt hate.

I've been lucky enough in the diocese I worked in that I have never come across sexism per se, but I do know that in some dioceses in the Church of Ireland there would be. This whole headship thing in the more evangelical bishops would be a problem. They are really not happy with women in leadership roles.

Sexual harassment did not feature strongly but the two women who discussed it with me urged me to "ask the others." It was their belief that women will still not talk about it because of shame and fear that they will be blamed or seen as inviting it.

I didn't feel safe and there is a particular man that I will not go and see alone and that's that.

There was a priest where I trained who declared his love for me and thought that was reason enough to touch me every time we were alone together. Of course, I couldn't say a thing. I was so young. He was thirty years my senior. Nobody would have believed me and I would never have got a church job.

This is related to the fact that women mostly still do not occupy the most senior roles in churches. In some traditions this was seen as a matter of time. Others felt that there were still barriers to women's promotion and that they were there on sufferance. Several women talked about being treated as little girls.

There's definitely the misogyny among a large section of the clerical people whom I have met along the journey of parish ministry. And also because I'm just a tad younger than many of them there's sort of a "nice little girl put in a box" thing.

We have to be little girlies. And it's quite difficult. I'm not a little girl.

Many women used the image of "being heard" for their gendered experience in church ministry:

The thing about ministry is that I have been so often at tables where I was naming stuff I just felt it wasn't being heard because I was a woman naming it. I felt that I'm ten years in ministry and if I said that I should be at the table for that conversation it's like "we'll get back to you."

It's not that we need to find our voice. It's that they need to listen. We are talking but we are not being heard.

One participant said that if she was at a meeting with male colleagues, instead of participating fully she would choose just one or two interventions to make because they could not tolerate any more or they would say she was "taking over."

A recurring theme was a sense of finding a place to minister and belong. Sometimes this could be done easily and sometimes women found themselves changing their ecclesial context or denomination or taking any role at all just to stay in a ministerial role.

And at the time I began to be aware of this call I felt there was no place for me. I couldn't understand why women weren't accepted into leadership roles. . . . It didn't seem logical to me, nor did I find any basis in Scripture for not involving women.

It's like we have to squeeze ourselves into impossibly small spaces so we can hardly breathe. And we're supposed to be grateful for that. When I look at the talent of other women—not even myself—it's such a loss.

There was some comment about how participants were treated outside their own tradition by ministers of other Christian denominations. Women reported these experiences in a detached and sanguine way.

I have had very strange comments initially but now I am accepted in the other—well I only have experience of the mainstream denominations and I'm accepted in those.

I remember going to a, sorry a Catholic church and arriving in the sacristy and the priest looking at me and saying, "And what are we supposed to do with you?" sort of thing. "And how do we address you?" Which I suppose was a bit of a surprise but I got over that.

[Regarding Northern Ireland as different from England] How few women in ministry there are. And how most men in ministry don't want to have anything to do with women in ministry . . . you certainly notice that this is a cold house for women.

There's a local minister fraternal in [place] to which I have never been invited.

(iii) Men

Women acknowledged that there were a few areas of ministry where it would help if there were a male minister available and that these were comparable with situations that male ministers might appreciate a female contribution. They identified work with young men and pastoral needs of men in this regard and also noted the fall away from church attendance among young men.

> I work a little with the couple of younger guys we have, but there are so many more young women and that is a much more natural fit—as indeed it is for the men to be mentoring younger guys.

> If I had a man curate it would be perfect but what can you do?

This coheres with the sense across the findings that women seek a shared ministry with men and acknowledgment of diverse gifts in ministry across the genders.

(iv) What Women Need

Women expressed various needs, including persistence, courage, and the respect of colleagues and others. They acknowledged that many of these needs were not necessarily gendered, but some were expressed as particularly applicable to women in ministry.

> Persistence. There's something from Lavinia Byrne, "It's your call, God has called you and you have to you follow his call." It's just simple like that.

> I think male ministers would probably really need to learn how to be courteous. I've seen bullying from Church of Ireland ministers toward female curates.

> I think that what women in ministry need is not just that men would change but it's actually ownership of our own journey . . . there's a huge need for us to tell our story, not as my odd and unusual journey, but as the reality of women in ministry.

(v) No Disadvantage

Thirty percent of the participants said that they had never felt disadvantaged by their gender in their ministry. Each of these women followed statements by acknowledging that others have experienced this differently and using the word "lucky" of themselves. These women were from most of the denominations represented in the study.

> It's not that I'm genderless but I've been very lucky in that it hasn't affected me adversely from—I've been able to achieve all I wanted to achieve.... I've been very lucky I've never been kind of censured.

> I can safely say, I'm in ministry now for [considerable number] years and I could say confidently that if there has ever been an issue it's been once.

> Why are women excluded? I don't feel excluded in the least. I think that's making it more of a team ministry.... In fact, they are called to do so many other things that we should be doing, can do and now do do, to free them for their particular ministry.

> Well I think in fairness to my denomination men and women are supposed to be equal. And I think that they are.

> I've been valued for who I am as opposed to what I am. In yes 99.9 percent of what I've done.... So I guess I'm one of the lucky ones who hasn't come across all that. I've been lucky.

(vi) Being Responsible to Act with Integrity for Equality

Women considered what their own responsibility would be with regard to equality and respect in the ministry setting. They discussed the elements of looking for offence and taking offence; of being provocative or standing up for themselves. They explored the element of "fitting in" to models and roles in ministry which have traditionally been occupied by men. Generally, women did not want to give their energy to promoting the cause of women but accepted that it was inevitable that they would find themselves adopting strategies or taking a position some of the time. This was an unwelcome fact for women who just wanted to get on with ministering but was seen as an occupational hazard.

> I know I have a responsibility to be a bit more radical too, but it doesn't seem to be one of my gifts to push out too far. I just find that

I, what works best for me is to sort of work underground and in a way eat away at the different relationships slowly, build up trust.

So, when I went into college I knew that not everybody agreed with my ministry—I did know that—but I expected them all to treat me with the same respect as anybody else and they did.

We can be our own worst enemies in a lot of ways. Why embrace what's rotten just to fit in? I don't mean men are rotten but why not be yourself? I think that can happen with women priests that they try to be the ultimate black suit, black shoes—that's fine if that's what they would have worn naturally. . . . But I do make—I try not to wear big earrings or something for services. I try not to attract attention, but you can't hide your boobs either so just be yourself!

(vii) Role and Expectations—Changing the Status Quo?

The theme of the male minister having been the norm and the effect of this emerged in many questionnaires and conversations. Women described the expectation that they would fit in to established ways of ministering and that this system did not allow for a new model to be imagined by women for their own ministries. They also expressed the concern that if they began to challenge this or to do some things differently they may experience hostility from others who were invested in the status quo.

I will say deep down it's not that any of these men—it's not that they don't want me—they don't realise what they're missing! And when I say that I mean that they are actually so fearful of alternative ways of looking at people; at family life; at young people; at ministry, they're so fearful of cracking the mould.

There's the thing of let's not let the women change the status quo. We're okay as long as there are only a few women who behave like us, but when women start to bring what I would consider feminine virtues into it of leading by consensus, that kind of thing, I think you might have.

And women and men work very differently and approach problems differently and so I think they just couldn't cope with me.

And the model we're given here is a male model. It's a male rector with a woman support behind in the kitchen and in the parlour.

I think, brilliant if people want to be deaconesses. . . . But my issue is with women being ready to support the status quo. And I think that there are problems there.

Where participants began to articulate what might be contributed by women to change this model they used words like "leading by consensus," "collaboration," and differences in the way they approach different aspects of ministry. This minister describes her prayer ministry:

I think the way I would naturally pray, is very different because I'm a woman. . . . I think the clergy pray with a very patriarchal, hierarchical view of the world. . . . I think my gender changes how I pray and because part of my work, part of my ministry is prayer then, that's hugely different.

The final part of this section should be left to an ordained minister who does not feel a need to pretend to know it all:

You can't possibly know everything. You're not a bloody builder. Unless you were a builder before you were ordained. You know, what would I know about gussets and gassets and fassets and fascias and I can't even bloody well get the words. You surround yourself with people who do know these things and I have builders on the vestry who know these things. I don't expect them to know the finer points of liturgy. . . . I do know some of my female colleagues who have had hard times with their vestries because they don't fit into the male model of being the tough kind of knowing all about fabric and finances. . . . If you weren't as sure in yourself it might be difficult to remain true to who you are and try and fit in with the model that they expect.

(viii) Domestic Life

All of the participants who were married and had families mentioned this dimension of gender and ministry. As has been seen in the section on difference, finding a balance of family and ministry as wives and mothers was challenging and participants acknowledged that it was more difficult as women. They expressed concern that their public ministerial life would not negatively impact their husbands and children. They also expressed the tensions in having to undertake traditional domestic tasks despite the demands of ministry.

And one night I was in and the oldest one who was only maybe four or whatever at the time said to me, "Mummy are you not going to work tonight?" And I said "No, N, I'm not going to work tonight." And he said, "But mummy you always go to work at night." I said "I don't always go to work at night." . . . Now my husband would never say anything, ever, you know and has never complained and he was sitting on the seat and he just looked at me and he said, "N, I'm not going to say anything. All I'm going to ask you to do is go and get your diary and tell me the last time you put your children to bed." . . . So I went and I picked up my diary and I looked, and, including Saturdays and Sundays, for five weeks I hadn't put them to bed. And I came back and I went, "I'm sorry." And he says, "Well only you can change that."

I was going home, and my husband was working full time, and I was washing, ironing, cleaning, doing all of that and still trying to do you know, ministry as well.

I have colleagues who have young children and I think that must be very difficult. It means that you have to have a very understanding husband and not everybody does.

I know I do more housework than N [husband]. . . . I know I did more child-rearing than N, so yes I think there are but I don't think those are peculiar to ministry.

[In terms of what she needs] A full-time cleaner and I'm not joking!

A small number of women expressed the view that they may have missed out on the opportunity to marry and have children because of the nature of their role. This may have been because of perceptions about women in ministry, or simply the unsocial hours which can be involved.

As Dawn French said in the Vicar of Dibley, "You don't go to the vicarage to have a wild time," you know? I was a holy woman of God you know? Nobody thought I was marriageable.

At a certain point you go, "There's twenty years gone." Now, I would know from dating that guys just can't handle that, that you're out. They want someone to take care of them so you know if you start off and you have that teamwork at the beginning you can work that through. But if you don't have that, then it becomes a difficult conversation.

Some women spoke about the particular challenges of ministry and pregnancy. This came up in terms of the system being created for men and so women's needs being seen as additional. However, when called upon the churches sometimes respond well.

> I hadn't told them I was pregnant. They wrote and said, because I'd asked our local parish priest. "I'm due to be ordained, what do you think? I'm pregnant." He said, "Just don't tell them. Do what Elizabeth did, hide yourself away." So, when they wrote and said, "We'd like to ordain you [at a particular place]." I just said, "O that's lovely. By the way I'll be six months pregnant by then." So they didn't bat an eyelid.

(ix) Money

In circumstances where women's employment was insecure or badly paid, and these were all Catholic ministers, there were serious issues about gender and money. Women experienced poverty and some found it difficult to get a mortgage or to support their family. They felt that male church leaders kept the money for themselves and made bursaries, courses, and opportunities easily available to other men, but not to female ministers. Most often women paid for their own training but were not guaranteed employment afterwards. Participants felt that they were treated as grasping if they raised financial issues whereas there was always a budget for their male colleagues.

> They were starting another course up north recently, two years and then you work in parishes voluntarily for four years, six years, and then we'll see if there's jobs at the end of all that. It's just not nice. It's not nice behaviour. It's mean.

> He sat myself and N down and said, "You can keep doing this but you will become, you'll never be well paid, you'll never be taken care of."

Women in other traditions expressed general satisfaction with their financial arrangements. They observed that promotion came more easily to men but they did not generally express the same financial anxieties. One situation which may be different in this regard is where a clergy couple who would normally command two full salaries are not in a position to earn these because of the structures and systems in the Church of Ireland. This puts them at a disadvantage not only during their ministerial career but also when it comes to providing for elder years.

It also emerged that women felt that men tended to be given roles where there was a more substantial budget and that women were seen as unable to manage larger projects. One woman had come from a financial background and expressed frustration that less qualified men were put into these roles.

(x) Support of Other Women

The support of other women emerged as an important factor. Many women acknowledged the influence and inspiration of other women and felt that there was a need for solidarity, given the sometimes challenging circumstances of women's ministry.

> Other women in [denomination]. They're a lifeline.

> I do try and support, and equally I wouldn't stick up for a woman just because they're a woman. Margaret Thatcher taught us that!

> [Women need] I think space to chat with women, having enough women ministers around and it was brilliant when N [a female minister from another denomination] was here and we could go off and have coffee together.

> Women need to be supportive of one another. I think everybody in ministry needs to be supportive of one another but I think that women in ministry need to be supported by women.

> I have always been the only woman in my context. That's lonely and I don't even go there with colleagues because they can't imagine what it's like.

(xi) Meeting Female Ministers in Person

Some ordained women described situations in which they knew there was some opposition to their appointment on the grounds of gender. They found that this opposition sometimes softened or disappeared when the person or group met them and experienced their ministry. They experienced this as daunting but told the stories with humour and a sense of God's grace. Many also described going to special trouble to include such people.

> There was an elderly gentleman who had said the words, "There'll be no woman in this parish over my dead body." And this particular

man said something along the lines of, "Well for a woman you're not too bad, I think I'll come back next week." And I said, "That's great just you do that . . ." Because I made a point of going to see him and he said, "I had a definite impression of a woman but I didn't expect it to be you."

Two of the Catholic participants noticed that Catholic clergy treat female clergy from other traditions with more respect than they afford their Catholic female colleagues. They attribute this to the Catholic clergy's respect for the status of ordination.

I couldn't believe it. He was describing her as a "colleague." I had worked with him for nine years and he would never call me a colleague.

7. Denominational Issues: "*In Our Church . . .*"

Participants spoke with a strong sense of denominational awareness. Their ministerial context was defined by church belonging. Similar responses came from participants in denominations which embrace equal access to all ministries. These women expressed a sense of satisfaction at belonging to these and while acknowledging challenges they felt supported and free in their ministry. Two women struggled to think of examples of gendered challenges within their denominations (Church of Ireland and Methodist) and could not.

There is evidence that women in churches which have gendered structural divisions of ministry face particular challenges. Here, although women were still very happy with their choice or call to be in ministry, church culture or limitations impacted on their flourishing in ministry and sometimes their personal well-being.

(i) Catholic Women

Catholic participants reported joy and satisfaction in their ministries, regardless of context. It was also clear from their contributions that context had an enormous effect on their ability to flourish in ministry. Although two Catholic participants said that gender had not negatively affected their ministry the majority of the Catholic women expressed their significant concern with the culture in the Irish Catholic Church.

These Catholic women expressed the view that there is systemic sexism or misogyny in the Catholic Church. This did not primarily emerge in relation to women's ordination but as a wider problem in church culture. Several of those interviewed used a particular word repeatedly such as "the system," or "the institution," to indicate the institutional church rather than the usually more positive context of their particular ministry. This was a persistent and dominant theme, and source of frustration and sometimes anguish. One woman described her experience of being limited in her role as a "constant diminishment."

> I just don't want to be in the system any more.

> I'm not too sure I love the church, but I love my faith.

> Lack of leadership in Irish RC Church. Total refusal to renew and move forward. So many people are just giving up and leaving—those in ministry of all descriptions are depressed and seeing out their time.

> A guy that had been the same year in me in college had done the same course and had done a pass degree in theology was asked to homilize. And I remember it just dawning on me that, "Oh my God that is because you're a woman." That actually you can do your best . . . you can be good at what you do; you can get really good grades and you can be really competent but you will always be. . . . So it was like this sudden realisation that actually that was the way—I can't even put language on it. That was really shocking for me.

Most Catholic women described the effect that this culture had personally had on their experience of ministry. This is summed up by this minister:

> You don't get to live your passion, you don't get to, to drive with your enthusiasm, it's always being tempered. . . . It's almost like loving someone deeply and going, "But actually they're off limits," if that makes sense. Do you know, they can only ever be a distant friend because I can't just say, "Look I'm passionate about this."

ORDINATION

All but one Catholic participant said that they did not wish to be ordained. Some had never been interested but most clarified that this was because they felt the whole clerical church culture to be unhealthy for both women and men. Many said that they would have felt the call to ordination in the past but now would not pursue it because of the church culture. The woman who did wish to be ordained said that she assumed that the ordination of women would not come about in a clerical-centred church.

> I never really bother about that because I'm not interested in that until the church gets itself sorted out about it and realises that you know, just because women and men are different it doesn't mean to say that both can't be ordained.

> I don't want to be ordained because there's a shortage of men.

> If I were invited in the morning by the pope I would say "no," because I know what they would do is the first ten years of women priests they'll all be put in monasteries and they'll all be followed around and made to cut their hair and all that baggage. And why in the name of the living would I take that baggage on?

> Would you want priesthood? I've never been interested personally. But I might like to be a prayer leader, do you know? So you know, I think other people might be wonderful pastors, and other people might be really good at keeping the administration of plant in shape. But we just have men who are geniuses and they do all of it.

> I would have done it off the bat as a young woman—but not now. But imagine what life would have been like if we had seen women in that role.

Clericalism and Clergy Training and Behaviour

Many of the participants described the difficulties of working in a clerical environment where the priesthood has been elevated, theologised, and strictly defined. Many described the behaviour of some clergy as domineering, disrespectful, and un-reflexive. They identified problems with clergy training and formation which left priests ill-prepared for collaborative ministry.

> And it's this inherent thing that God is held in some way, released through these men. Which is just mad. I think that most of the guys within the system are utterly unaware of the impact of their behaviour. And when you name it they get hurt . . . it's that lack of awareness. Privilege—it's privilege.

It's *their* Mass. That's the mentality . . . I don't think it's meant to be like it's . . . my Mass and I'm the king and I'll tell you what to do, I think it's fear. I think it's fear that if I'm not in control of everything that's going on something will snap.

Poor formation of even the youngest clergy in relation to team ministry, to delegation; to trust laity; crippling effects of administrative duties for parish priests means far less time for promoting pastoral/developmental ministry. Overt misogyny in some situations.

The majority of Catholic women expressed their appreciation of their ordained colleagues. They mentioned those who prioritised team; involved them in ministry and leadership and offered personal support. They expressed sympathy for clergy who suffered from the "system," and who were disappointed in the church and said that clergy needed support and ongoing formation.

Two women made the observation that clergy nearly never openly supported and promoted women's ministry because they believed it would affect their prospects. They may offer their tacit or private support but would never speak out and expect women to understand that.

They won't do it in case they get posted to the back end of beyond! They don't see it as their job to speak out about women. Even the "good guys." If you support us, say so. They have watched me get destroyed and said nothing. If it were the other way around I would have risked my neck to help them.

In general women experienced fewer problems and obstacles in their ministry when they did not work directly with clergy. Roles such as chaplaincy, female religious orders, or spiritual accompaniment appear to provide more freedom for women to minister and hold positions with more seniority and influence. Women who worked in parish or diocesan roles where they worked directly with clergy, or reported to priests or bishops, reported more frustration and offered more examples of being undermined, undervalued or bullied.

CLERICAL CHILD SEXUAL ABUSE

The topic of the crisis of child abuse came up as part of the landscape of the Catholic Church in Ireland. One Catholic participant mentioned it in relation to a more closed environment and defensiveness among church leaders. Here she noted that instead of the atrocities committed by priests leading to a greater role for women, they led to a sense of victimisation in the clergy and a sense that they could only trust each other.

One person described a sense of being caught in the middle and another said that many people confided in her but the leaders were somewhat protected from the responses of church members.

> I think they all should have resigned, all those bishops, all of them. But I was very shook because whoever I turned to I had my back to someone else. . . . I felt like crying all the time because every time I tried to say something that was helpful I hurt someone.

> The priest cried in the pulpit, for the awfulness of it and for himself, but I was the one people came to. They didn't discuss it with him. I don't think the bishops and clergy will ever get it, and instead of being more humble and open now, they are worse.

This crisis also had financial implications for the church. This also had an effect on female ministers.

> During the height of child abuse revelations I was asked to take a pay cut so my employer could pay out compensation to victims. He had a daily cook, cleaner and secretary, I had n. children to feed and clothe. Talk about paying for the sins of the fathers. . . . I said "no" and they didn't renew my contract. Over time you see that they are morally bankrupt. They can't sink any lower.

Women also drew attention to the fact that in the Catholic context that ordained ministry is always male and lay ministry in formal roles is most often female. Therefore, there is the dilemma of a blurring of gender and the lay/ordained roles. Outside the religious congregations, men are always in charge simply by the fact of being men. Women are always dependent on men for what can and cannot happen in their ministries. One woman believed also that lay men are more valued than lay women and are paid more for their ministries.

Many Catholic women spoke and wrote about what needed to happen in the Catholic Church regarding women in general and specifically about women's ministry:

> I think that the institution, the clerical institution, don't value women's voices enough.

> Maybe we need to get you know louder, stronger about pushing back. I mean we need our voices to be heard because in most cases we are actually hearing more of what's going on for the real people as opposed to what the institution thinks the people need.

Most of the Catholic participants were single women or members of religious congregations and this is generally true of women in Catholic ministry in Ireland. Two of these mentioned that they thought that it would be impossible to minister in the Catholic setting if married with a family because of the instability of employment and unsocial arrangements. They noted that the model of ministry was single and celibate. This was borne out by one married participant:

> My husband has never been invited to any dinner, or anything at work. We don't feel our marriage is acknowledged or respected. I have never earned enough to support my family. That has put the onus on him. My family are constantly on the edge financially. This has affected my marriage and we are constantly worried about when the children are older and need college and opportunities because it's just not there.

(ii) Women from the Church of Ireland and Protestant Churches

These participants were generally more content with their ministerial setting and it is clear that the reasons for this were fewer external restrictions and also a more egalitarian church culture. Members of the Methodist Church, the Church of Ireland, and two smaller denominations were most confident that their denomination supported equality in ministry. Many Protestant participants did, though, acknowledge theologies prevalent in some sections of their churches which did not fully support their ministries.

Those ordained in Protestant traditions acknowledged that it was "part of the job" to work alongside colleagues who did not support their ministry. None complained about this and some complimented these men for working with them. Many felt that, although some congregation members had initially opposed their appointments, some of these came around when they met them in person. However, others withdrew and worshipped elsewhere.

> The person who is now in [role] would not agree with the ordination of women but I sit around the table with him and he treats me just the same as anybody else.

Part II

Presbyterian Women

Some Presbyterian women described their assembly as inclusive of women but very much heard in the voices of men and noted that most senior roles are occupied by men. Some reported that church leaders whose theology leads them to oppose the leadership of women may wish to reverse the decision to ordain women in the Presbyterian Church. One woman described this as "living under a shadow." Other Presbyterians did not feel that this was a real concern but expressed the hope it would not come about. Another observed that there is a polarisation and that where there used to be room for people with diverse views this was now less the case.

> The rumour went around then that recently that they were going to try at this last assembly to bring forward that we shouldn't be ordaining women ministers any more. So that's in the air for our church at the minute. . . . The theology has got more and more and more fundamental in these days. . . . So free thinkers are being made go that way or that way. You're not able any more to kind of understand both and accept it.

Several women identified a change in the training college ethos. This is summarised by one minister:

> I think that perhaps in the last couple of years a course has been instigated for deaconesses. And so I think that there are problems of perception for people around the idea of women in ministry. It's okay for women to be deaconesses but it's not okay to be in ministry.

It was acknowledged among Presbyterian women that some who would be active in promoting the status of women may then be identified with this cause to their cost.

> There she goes again.

There is awareness of the need for solidarity with women but the overall hope is that a time will come when this is no longer necessary. There is a commitment to working together and finding ways forward.

> I love to preach and feel gifted in the area of preaching and in our tradition preaching is a big deal! It's also the area that the more conservative guys are really uncomfortable about—they have moved a long way from the old patriarchal days and are, I do believe, doing their best to include women, as long as it is not in

preaching to men and having authority over men. The issue for me then is that this whole network develops of women's meetings and women's preachers just for women, especially in America. I'm all for a bit of that but I think the Bible is pretty clear that we are all meant to be in this together, men and women.

It is clear that the question of gender is multilayered with cultural and historical influences, and this is even more true in the case of each denomination. Participants responded to these topics with great seriousness and sincerity and these areas were notably lacking in angry words or bitterness, even when painful episodes were shared. It was clear that women had already thought deeply about these matters and were aware that there were further obstacles to overcome, sometimes on a daily basis. While women expressed a certain weariness about having to deal with gender at all, there was also a sense of resignation and perseverance if this was what was necessary to fulfil the roles to which they were called.

So, after compiling these many-layered findings it remained for me to consult with a group of female ministers to ask what they made of them; what rang true or not, and whether there were any areas which were not covered. It is to this conversation that I now turn.

4

The Research Gathering
Reflecting on the WMI Report Findings

To TEST AND ENRICH this research, it was important to share the findings with female ministers, both those who had participated and others. While there are a limited number of female Christian ministers in Ireland the field encompasses many perspectives. It includes the inherited tensions in the north and south of this island. It also includes the various Christian denominations and how they are lived in each circumstance. There are also theologies which some denominations share despite other differences. There are expressions of the Christian church in Ireland which do not consider themselves denominational. As has been seen in the findings, when the issue of gender is added to these elements there is quite a complex range of experiences within a seemingly narrow cohort. It was invaluable, therefore, to invite both participants and other stakeholders to participate in responding to the findings. These findings represented the first insights into an under-researched group. I decided to limit the responding group to the same category as those who participated in the research. Working with a group of stakeholders on responses to this report gives a deeper and richer texture to this final account, and a more nuanced indication of areas for future research.

I sent out an invitation with an original response of twenty-two people. Of those, fifteen finally made it to the gathering. The participants donated their own time and travel expenses, and some were able to source or partly source this from their churches or employers. The group who came for this gathering was made up of some women who had responded to the initial research via questionnaire or interview, and some who had not. Some were very familiar with the project and some had just heard of it. All had read the second part of the report which included findings, questions arising and the conclusion.

These participants came from five Christian denominations and included women from a variety of ministries including religious life; ordained ministry; spiritual accompaniment, formation, and diocesan leadership. The process was very simple. The first session invited women to share their personal responses to the report: what stood out; what resonated; anything which they questioned and any gaps. The second focussed on the three main areas of questions which arose: the issue of models of ministry; call and discernment and ecumenism. The final session was for women to raise other areas of importance. The discussions were rich, informed, and nuanced, and there was generous sharing in an atmosphere of support and solidarity. Time was limited and many of these rich exchanges could have yielded even more insight, but the members of this group made every minute count.

To record to the reflections of the group I depended on my own notes; feedback sheets which were provided to small groups, and notes which were taken by individuals. Some people also emailed me with particular responses during the week following the gathering.

I wanted the participants to enjoy their time of meeting together so as well as allowing some social time I also allowed for several slots of shared prayer or worship, should people wish to participate in them. In the weeks leading up to the gathering I invited diverse participants to prepare lead prayer and music for those occasions. In fact, not only did they do this, they did so very much in keeping with the nature of the gathering in response to the report, so I have included some of the elements of the worship in this chapter.

There was considerable overlap among the various areas discussed so I have summarised them in themes. As well as answering questions, the discussions themselves gave rise to more questions which will be of interest for further research and which I will include in my reflections in my conclusion.

Women who came to the gathering enjoyed one another's company and found the experience refreshing and affirming. They decided to share contact details and keep in touch. This reflected findings around solidarity between female ministers. In addition, there was a particular ecumenical dimension to the conversation. Participants shared and compared the experience in their various traditions. This gave rise to learning, laughter, discovery, and solidarity. Although the stated aim of the gathering was discussion about the research project and this was very much fulfilled, participants reported a space of refreshment, friendship, prayer, and personal encouragement.

For clarity, where I am describing women who participated in the research I will call them "participants." I will call the women who participated in the research gathering "responders."

GENERAL RESPONSES

The general response to the report was very positive. Responders agreed that all of the findings were "recognisable." Where something was not their direct experience they agreed that it was certainly present in the experience of female ministers in the churches. They noted that the findings conveyed a sense of contentment in ministry and positivity about the roles occupied by the participants. They felt affirmed that the voices of women in ministry were present and made public, and that questions were raised about the culture that female ministers, particularly women in ordained ministry, had inherited.

Some responders expressed some surprise at the sense of shared experience. One woman reported that experiences which had seemed highly individual, perhaps even verging on the peculiar, turned out to be shared experiences with other women in ministry. Where there were significant differences in experience there was curiosity and support and a sense of solidarity.

The discussions were deep and wide-ranging. I have compiled responses here using ten themes: power; models of ministry; call and ministry; gender and women's experience; clothing; sexual harassment; naming God; identification; worship and liturgy, and gaps.

POWER

An aspect of the report which stood out for many of the responders was that of power. In my conclusion to the report I observed that the female ministers did not express any personal ambition for promotion, power, or influence. It was surprising to me that a group of women in leadership and who were highly educated and able did not express personal ambition at all.

The responding group wondered whether this was really true. Was this because female ministers were not interested in personal advancement, or power or could it have been for other reasons? Was it because the desire for power is associated with a historically male understanding of power? This was described as an understanding of power as "power-over." Another reason may have been that women were not expected to seek positions of authority or influence, and that they would have felt reluctant or presumptuous to have done so. Another reason posited was that women may feel that there was an expectation that they would be junior or achieve less. This reflects the findings where research participants said that less was expected of female ministers. For responders this possibly reflected an internalised sense of gendered expectation which may lead women to be "meek and mild," and self-denying.

The discussion about power led to a question about how power is conceived in the churches. Is the power exemplified by Christ "power-over," or something different? Could female ministers embrace a model of power which is based on the praxis of Jesus which eschews domination and promotes service? This is still power and brings influence and responsibility but is not self-seeking nor potentially destructive.

This may be linked to wider cultural questions and to the educational formation of women in particular and of society in general in terms of expectations placed on women, especially by women. Cultural inheritance can be difficult to acknowledge. Responders acknowledged that any form of power can be abused. Where there is a contract and accountability this can be a form of power "in service."

An insight and agreed understanding here was that women are the gender that knows what it's like to be excluded. At a very deep level women "have the code" of those who are excluded and can use their power to include or show awareness of those on the margins. This is a kind of power which is rarely seen. Women can use this power to be part of a positive change in the churches by including and listening to those on the edge and noticing where privilege is exercised.

MODELS

A clear result in the research findings was that women felt they had inherited a "male model of ministry." It was not clear what characteristics defined this or what specific effect it had. Responders agreed with this view and discussed what it meant to them. There was agreement that the model may be patriarchal rather than male as such, though these in many instances these meant the same thing. They agreed with participants that seeing men in ministerial roles had the effect of embedding the idea that these roles belonged to men. They agreed that seeing women in ministerial roles changes these perceptions but very slowly. The presence of women in ordained ministry in some churches also changes perceptions and expectations in other denominations.

There was a proposal that a male model can be summed up by the expectation that there is one perfect person in whom all gifts reside, rather than a limited person, gifted in her own way, who balances ministry with including the gifts of others and family commitments. The male model is performative and expects support from others. It can be centred on self. An alternative would be focussed on the gifts of the community. A male model of ministry sees other people as resources to be used for functions associated with the will of the leader. In this model other people are foot soldiers in service of the leader's command. In alternative models there is collaboration and shared leadership.

It is historically true and still numerically the case that ordained ministry is male and lay Christianity is female. The role of the clergy wife is also embroiled in this modelling and this group of women is worthy of its own research. Where both members of a couple are clergy the expectations of clergy wife cause particular problems.

In answer to the question of how the contribution of female ministers is already changing models of ministry the responders said that the fact of women's presence brings a difference. While not wishing to ascribe particular qualities to women, the presence of women themselves is an essential part of change. This may also bring about resistance as there will inevitably be some resistance to any change. Change comes very slowly and gendered change may be the slowest of all. Responders agreed that "we are part of the change but we are not there yet."

The call of women to ministry in Christian denominations represents change. The responding group agreed that the ministry of women is a sign of transition for ecclesial communities. It is well documented that institutions find change and transition extremely difficult and this can mean that individuals who feel they are losing something might visit their pain and frustration on female ministers.

There was also a discussion about the maleness of Christ in terms of call. If a person is called by a male figure to serve in a faith tradition with this male figure at its centre, and especially when his maleness is interpreted as important or normative, it will be very much more difficult for a woman in operate in this setting. For a woman to operate to her full potential and in a leadership role is even more challenging.

CALL AND MINISTRY

These responders agreed that call was a very important aspect to ministry, for both women and men. They expressed a view that it was experienced differently by women insofar as women often needed to feel a strong sense of legitimacy of call before putting themselves forward for ministry. More was at stake for women who answered the call to ministry especially in ecclesial environments which did not support equal access to ministry roles. This group wondered whether women were more likely to resist their call for longer where it may be deemed unacceptable to others. They also observed that women may have more fear about letting down other women if they made natural mistakes or were imperfect in their ministry. They felt that this was discouraging for women and it was wearing to constantly be expected to be different, interesting or a "breath of fresh air."

The question posed in the report of how the call to ministry is discerned both by women and by the community to which they belong was explored. This seems to be straightforward where women are admitted to all ministries, but what about churches which do not accept women's ordination and leadership? Responders discussed whether ministry is given by a community, whether the call is "owned" by the woman or by the church. What is God doing in calling women to ministry, especially into roles which were not "allowed?" How can this call be discerned? They made the distinction between being called and being sent. The call may be the responsibility of the Holy Spirit but it is the role of the ecclesial community to accept and recognise the call and to send the individual into ministry. The identity of the community, of "who we are," gives rise to the discernment process and the recognition of the community both empowers and strengthens ministry. Who represents "who we are" in the discernment of the church is a crucial issue which affects women, especially where the decision makers are exclusively male. Here the boundary between ordination and other ministries is somewhat blurred. Responders acknowledged the need for a diversity of ministries without hierarchy, and then the whole range of ministries and people in them could more easily flourish.

The group resonated with the experiences described in the report and reflected that in their own ministries their call was a sustaining factor which was a source of passion and joy in daily ministry. They agreed that it was primarily a call to discipleship which was expressed in their lives as ministry. Where life presented difficulties, their experience was that the power of their call in their lives constantly created different paths. Here the image was used of a river which flowed over and around stones, turns, banks and other obstacles.

The responding group explored why there might be a greater number of single women in Catholic ministry. Is this because God mostly calls single women; because once they are in ministry women find it harder to find a partner, or because the circumstances and arrangements for working in ministry make it difficult for a woman who is married with a family to continue? Responders did not believe that God preferred or mostly called single women and attributed this statistic to the other two circumstantial factors. They also noted that because of the factor of celibacy as a norm for ministers in the Catholic tradition, a married woman may have further obstacles to overcome in order to fit in to the ecclesial culture. Anecdotes were told about married women who had become ministers of the Eucharist being told not to "engage in marriage relations" the night before Mass. While this is not the teaching of the church, people noted that it was in keeping with the church's cultural suspicion of and distaste for sexual activity.

The research participants who were married with families, mostly ordained women, noted that the extra domestic work they did probably mirrored that of women in other professions. Some noted that the flexible nature of the work meant that they could collect their children from school and plan to be present at important times such as parent teacher meetings, birthday parties and so on. The key concern for married Catholic participants was financial. They managed the hours and commitment but the insecurity of contracts and payment made their involvement difficult to sustain and put significant strain on family relationship.

There was a discussion about developments in Catholicism in which parish communities appear to be starting to take more responsibility. Responders noted the contribution of one participant who observed a misunderstanding between definitions of vocation and ministry. It was agreed that a deeper exploration of these understandings would benefit all the churches. As a general rule, it was deemed that churches had a duty of pastoral care for all people who present themselves for ordination. Where people were accepted this was generally the case. Where they were not, the pastoral care came to an end with their rejection.

GENDER AND WOMEN'S EXPERIENCE

A significant part of the findings dealt with the area of gender and responders had several observations to make. They observed that gender issues in the churches were more pervasive than the ministry of women, and that issues around women's ministry were probably an expression of more deep-seated gender issues which were present both in church tradition and wider cultures.

A particular area which also emerged under the theme "naming God," was that women's experience and perspectives on the world have not been included in church liturgy and tradition. They observed that this is also true of LGBT people and other minorities. However, women are not a minority group and, within Christian churches are usually a majority group.

Responders observed that what is often recognised as "spirituality," emerges from monasticism and is male in origin. They noted the absence of spiritualities emerging from women's experience such as pregnancy and motherhood. The version of "femininity" espoused in theology and churches is prescriptive and facilitates male control of women and their contribution. Women's bodies are seen as particularly suspect. This is seen in interpretations of the figure of Eve in Christian exegesis. A responder noted that baptism is an appropriation of the female experience of birth but is seen as better and more necessary—being "born again." Others noted that this was supported by theologians who express the view that the Christian sacramental tradition appropriates and improves upon activity which is predominantly female such as feeding, reconciling, serving and healing.[1]

On the other hand, male experience and male bodies are revered as holy. In Catholic tradition the hands of the priest have been seen as sacred. Responders observed a dualism in Christian theology which disconnects body and spirit and that spirit is associated with maleness and superiority and body is associated with femaleness and inferiority. Married women who are in sexual relationships are particularly undervalued because of this. This can be seen in the practice of churching which took place in Ireland

---

1. See Ross, *Extravagant Affections.*

until quite recently and is now more often seen as a blessing for the mother or as a prayer of thanksgiving for a safe delivery.

Responders discussed the area of silence. They observed a culture of silence in the research findings. Women do not take up equal space in the churches. They are resigned to silence and exclusion. The biblical exhortation of women to silence has been detrimental to women's participation in the churches and especially in ministry. Responders noted that participants said that male colleagues did not speak out about the oppression of women in the churches and asked what it would be like if it were the other way around. In this case the silence of men reinforced the silence of women.

CLOTHING

A further dimension of this conversation was the issue of clothing which emerged in the report. Participants had discussed wearing clerical dress, the wearing of black, of painting their nails, and so on. What should female ministers wear, and did it matter? This was explored energetically at the gathering. What does it mean for a woman to wear clerical dress, specifically the collar? Is it different for women or men? Should there be any uniform required for ministry? If a collar or habit is not worn is there an expectation of "appropriate dress," and what might that mean for women and does this differ? The wider issue of theology and sexuality was touched on here but it was not possible to explore it further.

Responders expressed the view that Catholic men are afraid of wearing the collar after the reporting of the scandals of clerical child sexual abuse, and Church of Ireland men can be reluctant to wear it as they do not wish to be mistaken for Catholic priests. Responders noted the research results in this area indicate that women wear the collar with the intention of it being a conversation opener, and a sign of availability for ministry rather as an expression of power or status.

There was acknowledgment that, in Ireland, the clerical collar is associated with power and status. When women wear it does it have this association also? Clergy responders spoke about the sense of being expected or contracted to wear clerical dress. It was described as a symbol with a personal story. It can be appropriated by the individual minister as part of their ministerial identity and as a symbol of service. Both participants and responders spoke of clerical dress as offering an invitation to people to engage with ministry.

There was also a discussion at the gathering about sisters wearing the habit. Some people regretted the fact that fewer sisters wore their habits these days. One member of a religious congregation, not wearing a habit, wondered why she should dress in medieval attire to carry out her mission. She did not see the habit as a necessary part of life as a member of a religious congregation.

DENOMINATION AND ECUMENISM

A particular characteristic of this gathering was its ecumenical nature. It may be the case that those women in ministry who were most interested in ecumenical dialogue were the ones who most wished to participate. Responders embraced the ecumenical dimension of both the gathering and the discussion. They reported that time was given in their small group discussion to sharing particular denominational experiences in response to the report, and specifically learning from one another how they operated within their traditions.

In response to the question of whether the findings indicated developments in ecumenical cooperation responders agreed that there was an overwhelming imperative for ecumenical sharing and cooperation. They observed that there are signs of growth in ecumenical cooperation but that greater initiatives around women in ministry would cement this in various ways.

They proposed that the visibility of women in other traditions was encouraging for all female ministers. It was especially helpful that diverse women were visible ministering in their own ways in varied contexts. This visibility is a key dimension to the gradual strengthening of the position of women in all the churches. Responders agreed that women are role models for each other across the denominations. This is true in the sense that women are inspired by one another's words and actions, but also their presence, just by being, and by modelling church leadership for one another. Ecumenism broadens models of ministry.

They suggested that women could model good ecumenical practice by making connections with one another locally; by making ecumenical cooperation central to their practice and by possible cowriting articles and reflections where possible.

Catholic women observed that they are excluded from the formal ecumenical conversation because they are not asked to represent their church.

These roles tend to be filled by ordained men who will present and protect the interests of the hierarchy or establishment, rather than by experienced and qualified ecumenists who are interested in dialogue and progress.

The discussion arose about attitudes to women in ministry in the various Christian denominations. For example, Protestant clergy expressed surprise that Catholic priests were courteous to ordained women of other denominations but were found to give less respect and recognition to female ministers in their own tradition. Here responders concluded that ordination was the key issue and that Catholic priests could "see" ordained women but that their female Catholic colleagues were in some sense "invisible" to them because they were not ordained.

There was an exploration of the possibility that the "wind of change" which led to the ordination of women in some traditions has slowed or stopped. Responders noted that the research participants expressed the view that the elements in the Presbyterian Church may be moving to persuade the church to reverse its decision to ordain women. They observed an increasing conservatism of approach to ministry, perhaps in part in response to matters such as sexual abuse inquiries.

A particular question emerged in the final session from a Church of Ireland priest who wondered whether something might be lost if Roman Catholic women were admitted to the ordained priesthood. Here she observed that Catholic women often described their ministry as a ministry on the margins. In this sense it potentially had a prophetic nature which was different to a ministry characterised by being at the centre, as ordained ministry is in all churches. While she wished to see ordination opened to Catholic women she wondered whether this more liminal ministry would disappear. Catholic ministers responded in agreement to this and further proposed that if women were admitted to orders, it would be important to try and keep this element, and that many women would continue to choose to minister as sisters and lay people, giving particular expression to an option for the dispossessed.

SEXUAL HARASSMENT AND HOSTILITY

The question of harassment was discussed at the research gathering. It had emerged in the research and those who told me about it asked me to ask others. There was not enough time to do this justice at the gathering where there was some sharing of the experience of harassment. After the gathering some women contacted me to tell me about the harassment they had suffered. This ranged from verbal harassment on a one-off or ongoing basis to individuals who had been physically harassed. The perpetrators in the case of Catholic women were ordained colleagues, and in the case of others were either colleagues or members of congregations. At the gathering a responder shared a link with the group which is an artistic representation of the verbal responses female ordinands had received at Cuddeston Theological College: Eva's call.[2] Several other members of the group had seen this piece of art and said that it resonated with their own experience.

There was some discussion about sexuality and power. When women take up spaces which have been hitherto occupied by men the opposition to this can become sexualised. This was exemplified when a churchman who expressed opposition to a woman's calling wrote to her saying that a "good f*** would put her back in her place." His opposition and hatred was expressed in terms of sexual violence, and this was not a single incident. This is shocking but can also be seen as consistent with some aspects of Christian complementarianism which claim that a woman's role is to be seen have value specifically in relation to men. It can also be seen to be coherent with models of power which are gendered in church and elsewhere. This dimension is also relevant in relation to abuse of women and children.[3]

NAMING GOD

An important discussion which took place at the gathering was about how women in ministry name God. This was focussed on an observation about the "narrowing of God," which a responder observed had taken place in church settings. Formal prayers and liturgies use a limited range of descriptors for God, preferring words such as almighty, powerful, or great. These give a particular impression of God which may reflect a male experience rather than a female one. Responders did not perceive any different naming of God in the research report. Although this was not the aim of the research

---

2. See www.artsrcc.wordpress.com.

3. While these serious issues can only be mentioned here they are critical questions for churches. Two helpful resources in this area are Victorin-Vangerud, *Raging Hearth*, in which she points out the possible toxicity of hierarchical family models in churches, and Egan, *Remaining a Catholic*, in which he traces the patterns of abusive elements in the Irish Catholic clergy.

it may have been a result. In response to this conversation I returned to the data and isolated words which were used of God.

Participants were not asked about their personal faith or about their perception of God but they did speak about God. The overwhelming majority of words used about God in the questionnaires and interviews were verbs. These included transforming, delighting-in; cherished; forgiving; and living. Only one woman used adjectives for God and the noun Presence was also used.

I also examined the data to discover how women described their discipleship or spirituality with the view that this may yield insights into how they perceived God. Again, this was not requested in the research and arose particularly when they spoke about what nourished their ministry.

These results may be very different if participants had been asked about their understanding of God or their spirituality. Just one participant said that she believed she prayed "incredibly differently to men." Others did not make a comparison. There is no clear evidence from the research that women perceive God differently to men. Certainly, there is a question here for further research, which may pertain to women and men in general as well as women and men in ministerial roles.

CONCERN ABOUT IDENTIFICATION

Regarding the fear of identification of research participants, responders understood that ecclesial perceptions of women might make participation in this project seen as somehow rebellious or disloyal. Those who were in churches where equality was valued and promoted had little fear of being identified. In churches where this was not the case women feared that they would be sidelined or seen as disloyal if they had participated in a project which the church authorities would see as critical of them. They feared that their job might be affected. Responders noted that this fear was set in an assumption that male leaders would behave in bullying ways. Another reason for this fear was that the findings of the project might hurt colleagues, even if they were true.

WORSHIP AND LITURGY

Prior to the research gathering I invited the women to volunteer to lead periods of prayer and worship. From the volunteers I asked six people from different churches to take on leadership and music, and they led our prayer times together in which everyone participated. On reflection it became clear that these worship times were in themselves responses to the research and to the experience of being women in ministry. While leaders were welcome to lead us in any sort of prayer, they each prepared texts and musicians complemented these with appropriate music. There was also a time for spontaneous prayer. Some prayer leaders consciously prepared worship which reflected the tradition from which they came. The final worship time was specifically designed around the themes presented in the report.

The prayer and Scripture texts can be summarised in terms of discipleship, response, challenge, and a concern for the world. Each of the prayers contained elements of both personal prayer and discipleship and ecclesial awareness through the use of Church of Ireland collects, Moravian selected texts, or prayers for the church. Each of the prayers also had an element of awareness of those in need, through prayers of intercession. The worship was therefore not insular, nor confined to the issues pertaining to women in ministry but was situated in the concerns of the church and the wider community in which it lives and serves. The prayer was ecumenically sensitive and participative.

In our vocation and ministry, we may be instruments of your love.[4]

Other prayer moments included Psalm 40, which invited reflection on our experience of ministry with its "ups and downs." There was an opportunity for the group to make their own contributions in prayer and reflection. A Methodist member of the group took the theme of "Follow Me," and reflected on Scripture texts of call and discipleship. The music choices were the musical adaptation of Isaiah 43 and then a hymn, "God Who Sets Us on a Journey," which calls for openness to new insights and a pilgrim mentality faithful to the gospel.[5] The prayer also held up elements of ministry and call and of the tradition of women in Christian ministry. We prayed the prayer of Teresa of Avila, "Let nothing trouble you."

The closing prayer, led by a member from a Protestant tradition, offered seven short Scripture passages which reflected the themes in the report regarding women's ministry. These came with short prayers and reflections between and led us to reflect on the tradition of women's ministry. The benediction with which we went on our way was:

4. Church of Ireland ordination service.
5. Dine, "God Who Sets Us on a Journey."

On leaving worship and making our way home, let us commit ourselves to living lives of welcome and hospitality, particularly to the
stranger and those who are not in a position to return the favour.
Let us ask nothing in return. We ask that we may go in peace and
love, and may God bless us all until we meet again. Amen.

It is clear that the choices of worship leaders formed part of the responses to the research in words, songs and Scripture selections and also
in the manner of leadership and participation. This worship is consistent
with the findings of the report, reflecting themes of discipleship, calling,
denominational belonging, ecumenism, and pastoral concern, as well as
joyful response to God's faithfulness.

GAPS

Some responders noted the absence of voices from LGBT, people of colour,
and Travelling Community. There may be participants from these demog-
raphies in the study but as they did not identify themselves in these ways
they do not represent distinctive voices.

Some responders also noted an absence of the voices of religious sisters in the research. In fact, religious sisters are very much present and this
is noted in the report, but they are mostly not treated as a separate group.
Where religious sisters made particular observations, these are present in the
report. The interview with Sister Margaret Kiely, presented in part 3, gives
insights into Margaret's ministry as a religious sister and social innovator.

A question arose as to whether participants differed in their responses
depending on the length of time they had been in ministry. This was a question on the questionnaire and came up with each person interviewed. In
response to this I returned to the data and did not find discernible differences based on the length of time in ministry. There were however participants who identified a change in their own perspectives over time. These
were Catholic women who said they had experienced a call to ordained
priesthood when they were younger and who now said they would not wish
to be ordained because of their experience of ministering in the Catholic
Church. One Catholic noted that ten years ago she would not be in the role
she currently occupies.

OTHER ISSUES

There were other issues noted in response to the report and which there was not time to discuss. These included the education and formation of clergy, particularly in the Catholic Church; expectations around the role of clergy wives; how informal forms of recognition might contribute to women's ministry and hearing the voices of young people. Responders agreed on the need for mentoring of women by female ministers, not only those preparing for ministry but all female ministers at different stages. A need was expressed for spaces to reflect together as women in ministry and a conscious solidarity among women denominationally and interdenominationally.

It was clear from both the findings and the research gathering that there was much more to say in this conversation. The participants agreed to meet in other places and other ways and with other people to continue it.

PART III

Interviews

MY THANKS TO THESE extraordinary women who shared their stories with me. Each was hospitable, gracious, thoughtful, and good-humoured. Their ministries are varied: Ruth was the first woman to be ordained in Ireland and her ministry is centred on reconciliation and ecumenism; Heather is a Methodist minister and was president of the Methodist Church in Ireland; Margaret is a social innovator; Soline's ministry is both to be a spiritual companion and to persistently challenge the church on women's ordination; and Pat is bishop of Meath and Kildare.

These interviews were informal and did not have a set series of questions. They vary in length according to the person and what they wanted to say. In these personal accounts it is possible to see many of the experiences and views shared by the women of part 2. Here they are set in the context of these particular wise and wonderful ministering lives.

Ruth Patterson

County Antrim, 2017

Rev. Dr. Ruth Patterson was the first woman to be ordained as a Presbyterian minister in 1976. Since 1988 she has been director of Restoration Ministries, a nondenominational Christian organisation committed to peace and reconciliation based in Northern Ireland. In 2001 she was awarded an honorary doctorate from the Presbyterian Theology Faculty of Ireland, and an OBE in 2003 for her work in reconciliation. She has published five books and numerous articles and now works as a retreat leader, speaker, and spiritual director. Her father was a Presbyterian minister, her mother a medical doctor. She is one of three children. Her sister was the first female surgeon across the north of Ireland.

A: Tell me about the circumstances in which you were ordained. What was it like for you as a woman?

R: Well, I was the first woman ordained in any denomination in the country so that was a particularly isolated road to travel. Prior to that I had finished working in Queens on the chaplaincy team with Ray Davey (Corrymeela). In 1971 I felt that I wanted to go and study theology. That was the primary aim for me, more so than ordination, because it would put into context everything that I had done before. I'd done a masters degree in community development in Canada prior to working with Ray, and I felt there was a need for some people who combined in themselves not only theology but also community work because of the particular nature of what was happening to us in Northern Ireland at the time. So I decided to go and study theology in Edinburgh.

At the same time although it seemed to me then to be a secondary aim, I applied to be a candidate for ordination within the Presbyterian Church in Ireland, knowing that no church accepted women at that point in time. They debated it, but they couldn't reach a decision so they sent it out to presbyteries, a bit like dioceses, to discuss during the year. In those years there were twenty-one or twenty-two in Ireland and at the end of the year eighteen came back for it and three against, and one confused. I think really, were they doing this a few years later, eighteen would have declared themselves confused, because you can pass all the rules you like to get people to accept something but the living out of it is a very different scenario.

Anyway in 1973 the church did vote to accept women as candidates for ministry and I came back and did my compulsory year in our church college and then was posted as an assistant minister to Larne and was ordained in early January, 1976. In Presbyterianism we operate under a system of call or invitation, so a congregation invites or calls you to be their minister. The big test was—I mean ordination was enough of a test!—would there be a congregation brave or foolish enough to call the first woman? And so I had to wait longer than most of my male colleagues. Maybe I'd been asked to go on a list and then they'd come back and say, "Would you remove your name because the fact that your name is on it is splitting the congregation?" That sort of stuff.

Whether I liked it or not, the whole question of whether women should be ordained or not was being judged on how one person performed or failed to perform. It was a very public thing. There was a lot of press coverage and interviews and a lot of judging and a lot of patronising.

A: What was that like, inside of you, doing that?

R: It was quite isolating. My father was a clergyman and was very supportive, a very open and visionary man, and he and I were great friends. A few others supported but most people stepped back and waited to see how it would go or how "she" would do. I had to wait longer than most of my male colleagues, without going into all the details, but then, in November 1977, there was a congregation who invited me to be their minister. That was Seymour Hill, a large housing estate on the outskirts of Belfast. This was at the height of the worst of the troubles. In Northern Ireland terms it was ninety-nine percent Loyalist Protestant working class, with all the problems you'd find in any large housing estate, compounded by a high degree of paramilitary activity. It was quite a situation to land into. It wasn't a very traditional church. They wouldn't have called me if they had been, so they couldn't say it's always been done this way because they didn't have an "always." I was able, along with them, to introduce things that mightn't have happened in more traditional churches. They didn't know that it wasn't happening elsewhere! Those years were hard but important. We managed to very quietly do a lot of cross-community work and cross-border building up of relationships.

A: Has that always been important to you?

R: Oh very. The whole ministry of reconciliation has been central.

A: So not only were you a woman, you were actually quietly challenging something very deeply embedded weren't you?

R: Yes. Those two things taken together were anathema to some of my male colleagues, especially the younger ones. I think a lot of men, when they get out and get the corners knocked off, have a little bit more wisdom as they get older, but others want a "pure church," and stick to *the* truth and a literal interpretation of the Bible and all of that is quite difficult. A number of years after I was ordained, maybe in the late 1980s, there was still a sizeable move against women's ministry. Even though our denomination was the first to ordain, there still was a sizeable feeling against it and they managed to get a conscience clause passed in our General Assembly. It allowed men who couldn't agree with the ordination of women to absent themselves from a service of ordination of women ministers. This was very dangerous because once you opened the door to that, you opened it to all sorts of things, which is exactly what has happened.

Today, our denomination, which is not the Presbyterianism that I was ordained into, or my father, has narrowed and hardened and tightened. I mean Presbyterians and Catholics were friends in Ireland at least up to 1798. We had the same penal laws enacted against us, and Presbyterians were very supportive of Catholic emancipation but that's another story. Today there's a sizeable move among the younger men in our church to try to get the church to reverse its decision on ordaining women, both to the ministry and to the eldership. It hasn't become overt, but it's nearly overt and it's bubbling under the surface. I think that part of the reason is that in a situation of uncertainty in the world in general, as happened between the two world wars and the Weimar republic in Germany, people look to an external authority who will tell them what to believe and say what to do—give them the rules and regulations and not so much heart knowledge. They want, I suppose, a "pure" church. If only they could step back and see it will never be pure while they're in it or any of us are in it because none of us are, but we're all part of a broken humanity. So that's quite hard and sad now because I've been ordained for forty-six years, and women elders have been ordained for ninety-five years in our denomination.

A: Is it about the Bible?

R: Yes, but it's their interpretation. I have a very different interpretation of Paul. For some of these men, their gospel is not the gospel of Jesus Christ; it's the gospel according to their interpretation of Paul, whereas if they really looked at Paul, he is actually very radical.

A: And regarding women in particular?

R: Yes, he was, and regarding that one verse which said you should be silent in church, he was writing to a particular group of people where there was a particular problem and he was addressing that specific problem. It wasn't for the church at large for all time to come.

A: So, you're saying you're picking it up in conversations?

R: Oh yes, and in what they will allow and not allow in presbyteries and in the way women quite often feel bypassed. But if you look at women in their actual congregations I would say by their fruits you'll know them. You know, they're doing a tremendous job. And it's not that we're all the same; we're not. Just because we're women doesn't mean that we have to agree. We mightn't agree with each other on a lot of things. But there are some remarkable women and it's tough for them.

A: And how is it felt by women who are ministering, who have been or-dained for ten years or five years?

R: I think for some of them who are more isolated it is very hard. We meet, not as a pressure group, but we meet about three times a year to share concerns, to share ministry together. Not everybody comes but you can pick up the sense that there is a definite shift toward this excluding. Some say they want to do what the Presbyterian Church in Australia has done. They've passed a church law that no more women should be ordained and they'll wait until the rest die out. There is one woman in training in our church college at the moment and I think that's because it is being made subtly so difficult. The people that are coming in to lecture and so on are not women and you can see that from the people who are entering—I hate to use these terms but just for shorthand—they're much more conservative.

Never once over all these years would I have ever been invited into the college to give even a one-off lecture. And yet ninety-five percent of the invitations I get come from the Catholic Church. My own don't want to know, and I think it's what I said earlier, it's because I'm a woman but I'm also hugely and deeply committed to reconciliation and unity.

A: And what is that like for you?

R: Well it used to cause me quite a bit of pain. Then I thought, "Don't waste emotional energy on that but go where the doors are opening," and by and large that's fine. You think you've got it sorted but every so often, when it's brought into sharp focus again, it's a bit like you've been wounded and you've got a scar over the wound, then if you're hit on the same place it hurts more than if you were hit in a new place. So that sort of thing will always be there but it's not holding me back in any way at all, and I feel such a huge sense of privilege. For example, some time ago, I was giving the annual retreat to the female contemplatives of Ireland and it was just such a privilege. So things like that help me to feel this is where God wants me to be. Now because I'm the age I am most of my Presbyterian colleagues think I'm retired and they've never really known what I've been doing since I moved out of the parish.

A: So, you have moved out of parish ministry?

R: I have moved out. I did fourteen years at Seymour Hill and then I came out to work in this organisation which was started by a few of us, Restoration Ministries. I've been full time in it for twenty-seven years.

A: Your ordained ministry started out headline gendered. I imagine that wasn't the whole truth for you, (R: no) you just felt the call. Would you say that your ministry has been gendered—for you?

R: Well to a certain extent, in that why do people have to say that she's a "woman minister"? She's a minister, so there's always that sense, especially in Ireland. It wouldn't be so in England where for example I think there are more female Anglican rectors than there are male now, and the Church of Ireland in general have far more—well it's the largest denomination on the island, and the Methodists haven't had the same trouble.

A: I wonder then why for the Presbyterian community it remained such a thorn?

R: It's very strange. I don't know. Partly the whole conflict here in the north. If people were already open, it made them more open. But if they were a bit tight, they became more so. And this is selling people short in terms of what the gospel is all about. That's what I would find much more difficult than the fact that they don't ask me to do anything, that people are being robbed of the fullness of what this is all about, and it's set rules and regulations.

I don't think that is so much theological. I think in its broadest and deepest sense, it's part of a wounded sexuality in that some men haven't really matured into a sense of who they really are. They're scared stiff of the heart because they equate it with emotionalism. Heart knowledge is very different from emotionalism, but also I think they're afraid and feel under threat. They don't know what to do with women when they come alongside. I'm not a feminist. I think a militant feminism is as bad as the other extreme. My primary identity is not whether I'm male or female, ordained or lay, it's who I am in Christ, and so is theirs, and in that we can have a togetherness and a whole, No one is better than anybody else but each contributes to the whole and we are poorer when one isn't there.

A: What do think has sustained you?

R: This may sound a bit clichéd but Dag Hammarskjold once said, "Weep if you must, but do not complain. The way chose you and you must be thankful." So there's this huge sense of the way having chosen me and sometimes it has been horrendously difficult. Not only within the institutional church but also in this organisation, because wherever human beings come together we're all broken. I felt it wasn't so much that I made a decision, but it chose me. Sometimes, when it has been difficult, for me the real meaning of faithfulness is not that we cling to

God but that God clings on to us. And so, even within utter desolation, there's this little flicker that God is there, this is life and I couldn't be anywhere else. So, when everything else is stripped away, I know I could not be anywhere else. And the older I get, I feel the less I know, but the deeper I go into mystery. I don't think some of my male colleagues here would understand that. I love words, and I've just used the word "understand." They couldn't stand under that. I know some men who do understand it wonderfully. One of the prophetic voices in our world today is Fr. Richard Rohr. Just amazing. He will understand that, the contemplative mind.

He would say, "If you haven't stood before great love and great suffering don't tell me you know how to pray." Maybe these people haven't had the opportunity and no one to lead them. It sounds as if I'm being awfully critical, I'm not, but I'm trying to understand. I think that comes back to something wrong in the selection, the training and what people are taught, and even how people are nurtured in their own churches and parishes.

A: It could be theological as well? What you think God wants of you? (R: Yes) Are you talking about a spirituality which might be adopted by women—a spiritual approach to being a woman in ministry with those particular difficulties?

R: The thing that will sustain you is to find that still point within. Because there's so much going on outside that would pull you in every direction. So my chief challenge, almost responsibility, is to be true to my own journey. Even in terms of the reconciliation work I always say to people the biggest reconciliation journey I will ever make is the one within myself. If I begin to even get that a little bit right, then any outer journey of reconciliation becomes possible. It will have its difficulties but it's gloriously possible. John Bradshaw says "we are not material beings on a spiritual journey we are spiritual beings who need an earthly journey to make us fully spiritual." And I love that because we are already spiritual—we've come from God and we're returning to God. In T. S. Eliot, the end of all our exploring will be to arrive where we started and know the place for the first time.

A: So it seems that your approach to survival is not necessarily an exterior—how you have to fight the patriarchy (R: No)—it's more how you respond to God within yourself . . . (R: Yes, yes.)

R: And actually, that becomes more and more important the further I go.

A: Does it make it superfluous then to ask if you knew then what you know now what advice you would give to yourself?

R: Well, it would be about being attentive to that inner journey, but looking back you don't know that and there are so many things you have to fight for to survive. In the early years I felt I had to be about ten times as good as the average man in order to achieve any position of equality. Not that I was ten times as good but that sense was there. I suppose I was a people-pleaser par excellence. Now I have a little more confidence in who I am and I don't have to, but then, compounded by all the stuff that I had to take when I was first ordained, I did try but you can't be all things to all people. The way some women try to cope is that they become a little bit more masculine. And I'd say, "No please don't do that." You know our call is to be fully woman; to be who we are. So, I mean, there would be loads of things I wouldn't do had I known. Hindsight is a wonderful thing, and retrospective revelation.

A: I'm hearing this vulnerable young woman. You must have had a strong sense of conviction. You transgressed by applying before the church had made its decision to ordain women (R: yes). When you look at women ministering, what it is they need?

R: They need acceptance from their male colleagues. Not all, some men are very supportive because they see. I don't know how I would answer that Anne.

A: So you think it's more than just an ecclesial or theological problem?

R: Oh yes, absolutely. In fact, if they were being very honest, I think it's largely not theological. And it has always been so. I'm no theologian and I wouldn't come down on either side because there's always more to discover and to learn: who God is, who Jesus is and who we are in relation to that. I love the suggestion that Mary Magdalen and Mary of Bethany were one and the same. Tradition tells us she was known as Mary mig-dala which means Mary the tower because she towered over the men in her heart understanding of what Jesus was about. And how, historically, the men who compiled the Scriptures have airbrushed a lot of that out. They've done it with the last chapter of Romans where they changed some of the names to make them look male. Even Luke who is regarded in a sense *for* women and the foreigner, while he features women they virtually lose their voice after the second chapter. Maybe he was trying to make the gospel more acceptable to the world of his day and it's been the same ever since. It wasn't until something like the sixth century that Mary Magdalen was described as a prostitute by one of the popes.

A: Should women in ministry in the Presbyterian tradition be getting together and saying, "We need to do something?"

R: Well this was a question raised this year. Would we need to be more visible and more vocal? One of our women who I think you would find it so helpful to talk to Katherine Meyer. Katherine is amazing and Katherine spoke at our General Assembly in a way that left everybody in awe. She's a wonderful person.

A: Is she advocating a campaign?

R: No, but in some way to be a bit more visible, to speak and be seen—otherwise it will seem as if we haven't put up a struggle at all and we're just wiped out. Not only seem but that would be wrong, so wrong and would be so detrimental to church.

A: Do you get a sense from congregations that they want women ministers, or not?

R: Some of them definitely do. If the majority of church members knew what was happening, they would be very incensed. But there are other congregations whose ministers have groomed them, both men and women, that women cannot do this. So while you're not meant to do it, some of them have let it be known that when it comes to the election of elders that there shouldn't be any women voted for.

A: And that has been a tradition for years? (R: yes)

R: But the minister can let it be known in such a way that you in the congregation should not do it, and you don't want to go against the grain and you'll not vote. Even if a woman is voted for it's almost too much for her to accept knowing that he doesn't want her.

A: So, it takes a certain sort of character to plough through with that (R: Yes, yes).

R: And it's not that women are militant. It's not that.

A: You say there's this dilemma between being wiped out and put aside (R: yes), and having to occupy a certain kind of resistance. It's not militancy but it might be deemed to be militancy (R: oh yes it would be). It's not a chosen militancy (R: oh no but it would be labelled as that).

R: You know that I just love that song from the turn of the century—the American women workers "as we go marching, marching, we battle too for men, for they are women's children and we mother them again." They were walking or marching for the vote but it's the same sort of thing. I mentioned a broken sexuality.

A: Do you think that women are necessarily damaged by ministering in a male-dominated church? Or can you be healthy?

R: I think you can be healthy but I think you've almost got to be broken before you're healthy. Maybe we all need to be broken you know, because then you come to see things a little bit more clearly. Richard Rohr's book *Falling Upward* says it's the first half of your life where you get the container right and the second half is about exploration, stretching and risk. You've been bashed about, and that's the time then to risk an adventure. I think you can be healthy, but it takes much longer and you have to go through that time. Thomas Merton said, "I will lead you through the loneliness, the solitude, you will not understand but it is my shortcut to your soul." Not everybody chooses to go on that journey and when hard things happen, we have a choice. Wasn't it *Man's Search for Meaning*—between the stimulus and response there is a pause? Not everybody knows that there's a holy pause. But it's in the pause that our redemption and our freedom lies. Yes, you can be healthy but it comes at a cost.

A; If you had a daughter would you want her to be in Christian ministry?

R: I remember my father when I was talking with him, he painted the darkest picture he could of what ministry would be like and then he said, "But if you still want to go ahead and I'm with you all the way." And he was. You have to be realistic as well as having the vision, and you can't be prepared for everything. My goodness, if I could have seen what some of it would involve I probably wouldn't have started out. I think that's a huge gift from God that we can't see the future. I love the verse in Isaiah where God says through the prophet, "I will give you the treasures of darkness, riches stored in secret places so that you will know that I am the Lord the God of Israel, the one who calls you by name." That really sums up the journey, when you find out who you really are. You're called by name.

Heather Morris

Belfast, 2017

Rev. Dr. Heather Morris is secretary of conference of the Methodist Church in Ireland. She served as the first female president of the Methodist Church in 2013. She has also been general secretary of the Home Missions Department, director of ministry at Edgehill Theological College, and served in Dundonald and Belfast Central Mission.

A: What drew you into ministry?

H: A sense of God's call. I was in Trinity College Dublin studying to be a speech therapist and I just began to feel—could God be calling me to ordained ministry? I talked that through with folks I trusted. I was beginning to preach at that point, training to be a local preacher in Methodist language, and somebody gave me permission to say I enjoyed preaching because I thought at that stage you really shouldn't say something like that, but I did. And so it was a gradual sense of exploration for me. And I think the piece of that that I sometimes took for granted and still do was that to be in an environment where that was okay. That being a woman was never—it actually didn't even cross my mind at that stage that because of my gender that might be something from which I was excluded. So clearly there was a nurturing environment there that I took for granted, which was a great gift.

A: And what were your hopes for yourself as you were beginning this journey? What were you hoping for yourself in ministry, this life?

H: Isn't that interesting? Even putting a question like that is interesting for me because it was just simply a sense of this is where God was calling me to be. I suppose as I envisaged that it looked like a traditional teaching, preaching, pastoral care type of ministry. So I suppose my hope was just to be where I sensed God wanted me to be. That was the beginning and end of it. The struggles for me were about relationships. I was going out with my then boyfriend, now husband. We broke up for a while. The piece that we couldn't see was how you could—so the question wasn't being a woman—the question was how would you be a married woman in the context of Methodism which meant moving.[1] Those were the immediate challenges for me and for us rather than a straight or simply a gender issue. Hopes for myself? I think it was about just simply wanting to be faithful, yes, and put that piece alongside it that there was a joy in activities, a joy in preaching, joy in leading worship.

A: Was ambition absent—you didn't see yourself with a career, you saw yourself as a disciple really? It sounds very impressive.

H: That's why I'm hesitating around it! It wasn't a big thing. It was more that my dad's a minister, and maybe there was a sense of this was where God was calling me. And maybe I did know what that looked like because I'd seen that modelled.

A: And so you went forward. And what sustained you then in ministry?

H: I think that relationship with God and other people; a sense of I just enjoy the work, I enjoy the call so it's a privilege. That sharing of people's lives which is just immensely privileged. I love preaching so I love just begin able to sit and study and share that. So there's enjoyment in that for me. What has been sustaining through the difficult times is that I've always been surrounded by great people; folks with whom I could talk things through either who were my superintendents earlier on in ministry and team later on with me. And so that sense of colleagueship sustained me. And then the other piece of that is in terms of relationship with God. It has been a learning curve of the things that you should have in place but which I didn't do early enough. So there has been a small support group of two or three over the last few years. This was incredibly sustaining for me. As I got older the things that

1. Methodism has a principle of itinerancy. *Constitution of the Methodist Church in Ireland*, section 7.

matter—I have a coach; I go for spiritual direction; and I try to build in retreats and that group of three or four. I didn't do that early enough.

A: What about challenges?

H: After leaving college I was stationed to the Grosvenor Hall which is Belfast Central Mission as a junior minister, and then had six years career break—we've two boys. After the time when the boys were being born and young, I was stationed to Dundonald in East Belfast which is fantastic. A few of people had genuine theological concerns about a woman being their minister but they were gracious, gracious enough to say, "Ach sure I'll maybe try," and that shows great grace.

A: People think they don't want a woman but then they warm to you as an individual?

H: Yes, that's exactly it. "I think I can talk to you." It's interesting isn't it? And I just think it takes courage if you've left on a principle point, to come back takes guts. And more power to them. So, I appreciated that.

A: So, it's overcome by graciousness on all sides really?

H: Folks are good and kind. I think as I go on, and I think probably because I'm second generation of women ministers in Methodism, I benefitted from people like Liz Hewitt, Ellen Whalley, and others who were before me or others maybe for whom there were more issues. So I think that my experience of Methodism would be of a community which has nurtured me now. We had a meeting this afternoon, our stationing committee, which is a committee that places ministers. And sometimes, I think not for a few years though, but sometimes churches when asking for a minister used to put in sort of coded things like we wouldn't want anyone with too many family responsibilities which is code (*laughs*) and I'm not the one at the table who ever has to pick that up. Or if a church actually says we'd rather have a man, and again they haven't done that for years, I'm not the one that has to say, "Actually that's not the way we work." There are men at the table who say that. I'm grateful for that sort of church family.

A: And how does the church cope with that serious theological objection, that people feel very deeply?

H: I think that again that was a debate that happened in the seventies before I was called. I think that my experience of Methodism is that we handle those things—we are small so there's a sense of family—and a sense of we'll grapple with this together but once there's a decision made, we'll move on with it. And that I think is how it happened. My experience of it would be that even with those, not many colleagues, one or two, who would have a difficulty with women in ministry or gradations of difficulty, and they are supportive, good friends. I know if I was in a context, especially when we were younger in ministry and younger physically, if we were in a context where folks were occasionally sometimes—interdenominationally there'd be issues being raised—they would be strongly arguing a Methodist perspective even if it wasn't theirs.

A: You were the first female president of the Methodist Church in Ireland. How did the presidency come about?

H: A Nominations Committee brings three names to Conference every year and then other names can be added "from the floor," and Conference then votes. I was nominated "from the floor" in 2011 and not elected. My name was then brought by the Nominations Committee to Conference in 2012 and I was designated for the 2013/14 church year.

A: What was it like to be president?

H: The church was wonderfully supportive and pleased for me. They, were also interested that it was picked up by press, etc. I don't think that my gender was a factor in people's voting, either way.

A: Do you see the Methodist commitment to women's ordination as an obstacle to ecumenism?

H: I don't! And my experience of other church leaders in recent years has been of nothing but warmth. And even other church leaders who I know would profoundly theologically disagree with women in this particular ministry, we've worked together, we've spoken together and there hasn't been an issue. From a Catholic perspective I've met nothing but grace and kindness so I don't see why it should be a barrier to ecumenism. Because there are so many things—I mean if you want to bring it down to things on which we differ why pick that one as an issue? Either you're working together, blessing each other and building each other up or you're not.

A: Is it theological? Is gender a theological issue?

H: I think it is you see. I do, I do. Why do I think it is? Yes, I don't think it's social, just in terms of just writing into context. Because I think those who would be complementarian, it is for them a theological issue about how we are created. Clearly gender is a theological issue but it is only one issue on which Christians disagree. So, ecumenism demands learning how to value difference, differ well and partner together.

A: What do women in ministry need?

H: Doesn't it all depend on environment? Or a lot I think. We gathered, when Diane Clutterbuck and I started here at one stage, it was Diane's initiative, and I sort of came in on her coat tails. We gathered the women Methodist ministers and Diane's a great friend of Ruth's so there's a great relationship there. Just to see—we'd dinner in the manse—to see was there a need for mutual support; how were people feeling, and nobody wanted it really. Not in a resisting way but just in the sense of "actually we're fine." So what makes that happen? I think that is because by and large because people have support structures and there's not a sense of opposition to the ordination as women. I could see how in that context you would need really strong fellowship with women and men with whom, you know you could pray and think and work in graceful ways.

My experience has not been an adversarial one so I'm thinking about what I need and what we need for ministry; what do women need beyond what men need? I don't want to be too simplistic but honestly nothing more comes to mind. Because we all need fellowship, we all need support, we've all got responsibilities in different ways and increasingly men have family responsibilities so why should that, why should we limit that to women? Actually we fall into a trap if we do that. Some people—oh challenge me Anne—but I'm trying to think what are the gender specific needs. And I hesitate to say there are gender-specific needs. Beyond an awareness that we all have that vulnerability that says we all have needs, we all need support and both women and men struggle with that I think.

A: You're not identifying a particular "all female ministers need this"? About what percentage of ministers are women?

H: About a fifth to a quarter? There are about 120 Methodist ministers in the act of work so not retired, so I would say about twenty-five-ish women.

A: And is there a greater number of women on non-stipendiary arrangements?

H: Interestingly one of the shifts we're finding is that fewer and fewer people are opting for non-stipendiary. Initially, certainly, yes, there would have been. We've had very few non-stipendiaries so I can almost think of the specific numbers. Our first couple were men, and then of a group that went through, three were women, one was a man; one woman, one man so it's slightly weighted toward women but not a lot more. No and ministry in part-time appointments is our other option, and, no probably more men and more often going on terms of health grounds rather than family responsibilities.

A: It seems there isn't that one gendered thing that there might be in other traditions.

H: No.

A: And what would your hopes be for ministry within the Irish Methodist Church?

H: And when you're saying ministry, do you mean ordained or the whole of ministry?

A: The whole of ministry.

H: If we're talking about that—and all my comments so far have been narrowly ordained, so in terms of ministry of the whole people of God my hope would be to see ministry of the whole people of God. That is a strong emphasis in Methodism at the minute, and a major paper came to conference in June past about lay ministry and recognising that. And recognising the ministry of ordained and lay side by side, not just in terms of resourcing church but in terms of in the world. So, a first step that you could almost see in the paper that came was thinking of lay ministry as only those who work for the church. Actually, then we saw that shift coming and said actually let's not fall into that trap. And seeing well actually the person who works in the bank and the shop and isn't working at the minute is engaged in lay ministry, so let's see the ministry of the whole people of God. So, my hope would be that that continues and goes from strength to strength. That's my major hope.

A: And that is according to charism?

H: That's it.

A: And what has been your greatest joy as a woman in ministry or as a person in ministry if those are different?

H: It's the people piece for me, let me think. Well the pictures in my head as I speak are of, when I was teaching here (at Edgehill College), students you just see on circuit now, flying. The other picture is Communion actually, in Dundonald, and you know, and that privilege of serving Communion to folks who you know are struggling to be at that table. Because of the personal tragedy that just happened or you know, just that privilege. So those pastoral pictures are the other ones that are there for me.

A: Is there anything else you'd like to add?

H: I think in terms of—again this is about ordained—I've just been noticing recently even in language, we're getting better even in language. It happened today you know someone was talking about the minister as "he," and I started thinking, "You know, that's really grating me," and why is that? It's because it doesn't happen very much (*laughs*). Folks are moving beyond, you know, I have to do this to be politically correct to actually it comes very naturally saying "he or she or them." So that's great. What else? I think that lay ministry piece is something that we are taking seriously. A part of that has been about a sense of "needs must." We've less ordained but I think that's going to change. But there's less ordained than we need at the minute, so part of that's driven by "whoops we're going to have to ask lay folks to—or acknowledge lay." So that's very interesting isn't it? And then alongside that is that acknowledgment of the richness of—so one of our emphases of missional discipleship and living every day as that seeps in and as that culture comes, then of course we're going to say . . .

A: Is missional discipleship significant for you at present?

H: Yes, it is. That's very meaningful for us. I like it because it does hold those two together. It's discipleship we need and that's part of Methodism but it has to be with a view to living it out. So, at the minute we need those words.

Margaret Kiely

Cork, 2018

Sr. Margaret Kiely is a Sister of Mercy who entered religious life in 1960. She was Principle Nurse Tutor at the Mercy Hospital in Cork before founding Tabor Lodge AddictionTreatment Centre in 1989, and later its associated halfway houses at Renewal and Fellowship House. She went on to manage a nursing home at the Society of African Missions in Blackrock, Cork. Margaret is now retired and does voluntary work as a tutor with Age Action.

A: What drew you into ministry?

M: I was born into a farming family in Ballydaly outside Millstreet town, the eldest of six children. I was ten when the youngest was born and there were four in between, so I was regularly caring for younger children and doing tasks around the house and farm yard. When I look back, seventy-five years ago now, there was no electricity, no running water, no radio, TV or telephones. Families were large and life was very simple. There were all kinds of animals on the farm so we milked cows, fed calves, looked after horses, pigs, and hens. In the fields we helped with saving the hay, picking potatoes, and hand binding the shaves of corn. Turf cutting was another task in which we as children enjoyed being involved. The threshing was the highlight of the harvest year. When the thresher arrived and the local *meitheal* gathered there was great excitement. There was food and drink for all the workers and treats for the children too. Machinery was scarce and there were little or no farm accidents at that time.

My parents were caring by nature. My grandparents lived with us and were looked after until they passed away. My mother had a sewing machine and made our clothes, taught us how to use it and would also do bits of renovations for neighbours. My father had a cure for sick animals and was available to help a neighbour when called upon. There was generally a great community spirit, where there was lending and borrowing and always people to call upon when a difficulty arose in the home or farm. The local church was the centre of the community and everybody attended Sunday Mass. There were numerous vocations to the priesthood and religious life in the parish. I had the opportunity to spend some time in Kenya a few years ago as part of my Mercy ministry. The simplicity of life there reminded me of where we were back then. So, in that kind of an upbringing I suppose I imbibed the caring element, the faith of family and community and multitasking came naturally to me!

Having completed my Leaving Certificate at the local Presentation School I decided to do a commercial course. I got my first job in a Cork hospital and the pay was thirty shillings a week. The office atmosphere did not appeal to me so I decided to apply for nurse training. I was accepted for training at the South Infirmary. This was my dream job. Classes were small; we were only five. We worked hard, had a half day off in the week and when on night duty we had one night off in the fortnight. We were paid £3 a month! Social life was nonexistent and the monthly bus fare home came in the post from our parents. Discipline was very strict but that appealed to me. There were no disposable materials, no plastics, and every item was accounted for, washed, sterilised, and reused. Strange as it may seem there was very little infection in those days.

I completed my nurse training and decided to join the Mercy Sisters. Having my nurse training was an advantage. I was with a group of novices some of whom had come directly from school. Others came from the Philippines where the Mercy Sisters had established a new foundation. Our contact with the outside world was limited during our spiritual year while we were being formed in the Mercy way of life. But we had good fun during recreation times and formed strong bonds which have lasted a lifetime.

A: What was it about the Mercy Sisters that made you feel "this might be for me?"

M: The Mercy Sisters managed the South Infirmary. I found them to be strict but fair and generous with appraisal of students when deserved. Our tutor was kind and caring especially when we students fell ill ourselves. The Mercy community lead a dedicated and structured life and used to say their morning and evening prayers in public in the hospital church. Though not actively involved in nursing care the sisters were a great example of dedication to the care of the sick. I felt a call to devote my life in this way as a Mercy Sister.

   Having completed my two years novitiate, I was assigned to the Mercy Hospital where I was to spend the next twenty-five years of my life. I was put to work in different departments of the hospital. I spend days and sometimes nights in different wards and in laboratory, pharmacy, laundry, kitchen, theatre and so I got good insight into the functioning of the hospital. I spent the next five years as Ward Sister in the children's ward before being asked to go for nurse tutor training in UCD. I found the course challenging as I had been out of school for so long. Being introduced to the science subjects for the first time was difficult but most of my class were mature students and we were in the same boat so we struggled along together. On completion of my training I was appointed as principle tutor. My predecessor had volunteered for Peru so I was put in at the deep end. The task of preparing classes and getting to know students and staff was daunting. I used to burn the midnight oil in my efforts to be one step ahead of my students. As time passed my teaching skills improved and I began to enjoy my teaching ministry. I got on well with young people and they were doing well in their exams. I thought I'd be there forever but then came another request from my religious superiors. The Mercy Congregation was interested in establishing a treatment centre, based on the twelve-step programme of Alcoholics Anonymous, for persons with addiction problems. I was asked to take on the onerous task of setting it up.

   Having agreed to accept this challenge I bade farewell to my students and to the sisters and hospital staff. I felt very sad leaving the Mercy Hospital and the many friendships and supports I had built up there. This was a new beginning for me. I had no knowledge of the twelve-step programme and my only experience of addiction was of the people who came into casualty intoxicated, and this was very often a negative experience. Having researched what was available by way of treatment centres in Ireland I realized there was no suitable training available in this country. Having prayed to the Holy Spirit for guidance I applied for training to the Hazelden Centre in Minnesota, USA, and was accepted within a few weeks. I joined an international class of twenty students who came from all walks of life. All seemed to have some personal experience of addiction and time spent in treatment centres. On arrival I saw that the training centre was called the Cork Centre and the local church was the church of St. Bridget. I was assigned to a unit called *Dia Linn* the name I was told "came from the Irish folklore when somebody sneezed, they were thought to be possessed by an evil spirit and people said Dia Linn—God with us." I felt that all those three elements were a great connection with home and confirmed for me that I had made the right decision. The Holy Spirit had guided me here to this great place. (I later learned that the Cork Centre was called after Kroc McDonnell, who donated the funds and St. Bridget's was called after Bridget of Sweden!) The staff and patients loved to tell me of their Irish roots and joked about being Catholic, Irish, and alcoholic!

As part of our class introductions we were asked to tell our life stories. I felt I was the odd one out as I was not recovering from addiction to alcohol or drugs. When I told my story, they told me I was in recovery from religious life! I was taken aback at the time but later I began to believe it! My way of life must have sounded very strange to liberal Americans. They used to say they were spiritual but did not belong to any organised religion. I couldn't understand that as I was a daily Mass-goer, come hail, rain or snow—and we did get a lot of snow in Minnesota. After a while I began to imbibe their spirituality. As part of our training we were all asked to attend some twelve-step meetings and to practise practice the programme in our own lives. This experience opened my eyes to the drug/alcohol culture and the violence associated with it in the USA. Thirty years later we are no different here.

Having completed the training programme in Minnesota I returned to Cork and to St. Mary's Convent which was renovated by the Mercy Sisters at a cost of €100,000. The building was ready but we had no funds and no staff to run it. In the meantime, we decided to change the name of the house to Tabor Lodge. Called after Mount Tabor it signified for me the transformation which took place in people's lives following treatment. One of my class mates at Hazelden who wanted to spend time in Ireland came to work with us and was employed by the Mercy Sisters for the first six months. Together we worked in preparing the way for the new arrivals. Sr. Rose took responsibility for catering and Sr. Austin looked after the house and grounds. It was not long until one man was referred for treatment. People asked, "How do we start the treatment centre with just one resident?" An American counsellor had told me, "You start with one person and bring all the staff into the group." So, that's exactly what we did. One patient and six staff all shared in group together and the experience benefited all concerned.

After a while the numbers seeking treatment increased and we got great publicity at the time from the *Irish Examiner* and local radio and TV stations. All were open to hearing about our programme as we were new to Cork as a residential treatment centre. I experienced fear and anxiety in the beginning, wondering whether we would be able to make a go of it, but at the same time praying and trusting in God and saying to myself, "Well, if the Lord wants it, it will be a success."

Sometimes we'd go from having ten patients down to three or four, and be wondering if this going to be the end, but gradually the numbers increased. We gave regular talks to students in schools and to parents and other interested groups. As the numbers increased then we set up aftercare groups which supported people after leaving treatment. My colleague from the United States did assessments and admissions while I was doing the promotion and staff training. Our chaplain Fr. Vincent O'Neill, SMA, was very skilled in technology and promotion. He computerised the office and wrote articles for local newspapers. All that was an area which was new to me and in which I had to become acquainted. A board of management was appointed and met monthly. This was a great support.

A: And where were you in all that? Were you comfortable, were you happy?

M: Oh, sometimes it was all a bit overwhelming but I appreciated the support of my community, staff, and board of management. I used to take the dogs for a walk early in the morning and I found that was a great way of reflecting, meditating, and planning. I felt I could pray better in the fresh air and in nature. The twelve-step programme was good practice for myself too, admitting that I can be powerless in such a situation, and that I need help. Coming from working in an institution like the Mercy Hospital where you have all the props and the supports needed and going to work in the community where you have little or no support was daunting. At that time, we had very little funding and so we had to do fundraising as well as lobbying government departments and public representatives. Members of the board were a great support and did trojan voluntary work in this area. Gradually the HSE and other funding agencies came on board and we were able to focus our energies on the care of our residents. I must say we enjoyed the company of the residents. It was rewarding to work with families and seeing them realising their own situation and how best they could help the addicted member. Family members were always very grateful for help and advice received. As the workload increased so did our staffing levels and after five years a new extension was added to the treatment centre.

After twelve years in Tabor Lodge I felt that it was time for me to move on. As a Mercy congregation we set up programmes and in time hand them over to lay management. I think maybe in the past we didn't move on enough. I went for a break to St. Beuno's retreat centre in Wales where I undertook a thirty-day retreat. It was an opportunity for me to reflect on the past and to identify areas in which I could still be of service. On my return to Cork I began the work of setting up the halfway houses—a form of extended care for young people leaving treatment. These were based on the model of care at the Hazelden Centre where young people lived in supervised accommodation and got counselling and training while practicing their programme in a sober environment. The need for such extended care had been identified for some time but the necessary funding was not available. Eventually, thanks to the Cork Local Drug Task Force for funding, a loan from the Sisters of Mercy and a property from the SMA Fathers both houses became a reality. The women's house was set up as Renewal in Blarney Road and the men's house as Fellowship House in Spur Hill.

Then I had some space myself but not for long. The SMA Fathers were looking for someone to manage their nursing home, so I made an application and was accepted. I took up the position and was there for thirteen years. It was a new experience working with older people. My patients were all retired missionaries, many of whom had spent their entire working lives in Africa. Some hadn't looked after their own health very well and a number of them were prematurely in poor health. I enjoyed going back to work with nurses and care assistants—I felt I was back to where I belonged.

While I was working in this capacity I had the opportunity to go to Liberia. Fr. Lee Cahill and myself were asked to take Archbishop Michael Francis back to Monrovia. The archbishop had suffered a stroke during the civil war in Liberia, and he was brought to the SMA house in Cork for treatment and convalescence. On arrival in Monrovia he was welcomed home by his friends and numerous public representatives. Next day President Ellen Johnson Sirleaf came to visit him. She thanked him personally for his services during the civil war. During my short visit to Liberia I witnessed the poverty and devastation caused by the civil war.

Over the years I have had the opportunity to serve on a number of boards of management, all of which have given me insights into the volume of work being done by the voluntary groups throughout this country. We would be a poorer place without such dedicated and selfless people.

I have always been blessed with good health but I did have breast cancer about twenty years ago and thank God I made a good recovery. Since then I have lived with an attitude of gratitude, for everything really, for the small as well as the bigger things. I am grateful to have a very supportive family. We're an extended group and tend to stay close and connected. They're all in Ireland and most of them in County Cork. Sadly, I lost one of my brothers last year.

Community-wise we live in small groups. We meet monthly in larger groups where we pray and share together and support one another. As we journey in this stage of diminishment we are well catered for and supported in our congregation of Mercy. We have spent our lives in service of our Maker and we are now experiencing the hundredfold in this life and hopefully life everlasting in the next.

A: What would you say has most nourished or supported you?

M: I would say community life, family, and friends. I have a strong faith and trust in God. Nothing happens without his knowledge. I have become aware of God in everything, in the people I meet, in nature and in life events. I am praying not for what I want in a situation but what the Lord wants of me and that I can accept whatever that may be. Often the answer I get is better that what I had expected. I have found praying the Scriptures in groups such as Lectio Divina is very beneficial. I also keep regular contact with family and friends.

I have been involved in a Bridge Club for many years and I find it a great form of relaxation. I work as a volunteer tutor with Age Action where we teach computer skills to older people. I have also taken up art and enjoy it.

A: Have there been times of real challenge or times that you've found especially a struggle as a woman in ministry, or as a person in ministry?

M: I can't say that I struggled because I am a woman. In fact, I found it an advantage. I've always had great support from both men and women. Whether it's in the hospital situation or elsewhere I have no problem asking for help, and have found that people are more than willing to offer help and advice when it is requested. I am reminded of one of the weekly exercises we were given during our training at Hazelden where we were asked to give examples of situations in the workplace in which we asked for help and the responses we received. It was a way of demonstrating our practice of the twelve step programme—God helping us through other people. There were times in ministry when I felt out of my depth but it was in those times that I became more dependent on God. Looking back these were often the most fruitful times of my life when I grew in faith and in my relationship with God.

A: If you could talk to women in ministry what advice would you offer them?

M: Have faith in yourself, your gifts and the contribution you can make. Treat all with dignity and respect appreciating each person's contribution. Trust in God. Acknowledge mistakes. Don't be afraid to ask for help. Have a healthy work/life balance.

A: What about hopes for the future?

M: If the Lord leaves me my health, I will try to do as much as I can, for as long as I can. As religious sisters we have been given a lot of opportunities over the years and I feel the need to give back in gratitude. In understanding and appreciating my gifts I become more willing to share. Speaking of gratitude, the author Frank Cunningham says that gratitude makes the person feel better emotionally, get sick less often, experience less stress, anxiety, and depression, and I feel I can be a witness to that.

Soline Humbert

Dublin, 2017

Soline (Vatinel) Humbert was born in France in 1956. She studied history and business administration in Trinity College Dublin and theology in the Irish School of Ecumenics. She married Colm Holmes in 1980. They have two sons. In 1993, with Colm and Fr. Eamonn McCarthy, she founded Brothers and Sisters in Christ (BASIC) to pray and work for women's ordination in the Roman Catholic Church, and was spokesperson for Women's Ordination Worldwide first international conference in Dublin in 2001. She is an active member of We Are Church Ireland (which incorporates BASIC). She has a pontifical diploma in spiritual direction (An Croí / Milltown Institute) and ministers as a spiritual guide.

A: What drew you into ministry?

S: Well, I don't think the answer is a what, I think it's a who. And for me, ultimately, it's the person of Christ. Jesus, the Christ.

A: And how did you know?

S: I was about seventeen or eighteen when that sense of being called to ministry came. It was a call to priesthood and it came in the wake of an experience of God's love. It wasn't what I expected at all. It's like an idea comes to you, you don't know from where, and it's very disturbing and won't go away and it doesn't make sense. It doesn't fit in but you can't get it out of your mind, out of your heart, and it's there, day and night, and you can't take a holiday from it and you think you are going mad.

I had other plans for my life. I was thinking perhaps journalism or law. Ministry was not at all on my radar, and certainly not priesthood, which was not on anybody's radar for a young Catholic girl. That's why it was so shocking to me, but it just wouldn't go away. It was like an inner, silent voice coming to me, and which had such authority, so I could not dismiss it. It was compelling; not an obsession but a strength; a quiet voice—very powerful and at the same time respectful. One wouldn't have had a sense of being forced or violated by that inner sense. I didn't know what to do with it. At one level it was in continuity with my faith journey, but so unexpected.

A: And was it certainly to priesthood?

S: It was the ordained priesthood and again that shocked me because this wasn't being discussed where I was in Trinity College at the time (1974). Later on, I understood it was being discussed, especially in America. But in the milieu where I was studying history and politics, it wasn't discussed at all. Ruth Patterson was ordained in the Presbyterian Church around that time but I'm not even sure I was aware of it.

I had a breakdown and part of it was caused by that. My whole sense of self was in question. I was carrying a secret which couldn't be shared. But later on, it came back. I tried then to express it. I said it to the one of the chaplains at Trinity who immediately suggested I consider religious life. I had friends in college who were considering religious life but never really got a sense that that was where I was going.

I remember meeting a Poor Clare sister in Assisi and she was talking about her life. I was very touched. She radiated her faith and her connection to God. Then I thought perhaps I would become a lay missionary with *Viatores Christi*. I investigated this but found that a degree in history and politics was not what they wanted in lay missionaries and I realised that I didn't have anything useful to offer.

You must remember as well that I grew up in a church in France which wasn't clericalized and where lay people had a lot of involvement. In Ireland there was nothing for lay people, especially in the early '70s. I would have seen my mother as the parish catechist and I was in a Catholic school but all the teachers were lay, so I had the experience of a strong lay involvement. I would have had an experience of an intellectual Christianity as well. My parents would have read Teilhard de Chardin.

It was obvious I couldn't do anything with it, so I decided to forget about it and do my best to be active as a lay person. I got married. I still associated priesthood with celibacy. When I got married, on my morning of my wedding—I don't think there's too many brides would think this—I said, "Well that's it now. Ordination will come for women but not for me because now I am married!" Looking back, it's funny.

Then I started studying theology. I studied catechetics first and then went to the Irish School of Ecumenics, and did my masters there with people like Ginnie Kennerley and it opened up my thinking. I would have had a strong ecumenical perspective, and this broadened it and opened up the interfaith perspective as well. I went back home with my masters. I'm talking about the early '80s. You were told your main vocation is to be a wife and mother. What else would you want? They wouldn't have said that to my husband! The ministry I did then was work for the diocese as a marriage counsellor with CMAC. I said, well if that's my ministry we can do this as lay people.

I put it behind me but it came back. The "it." That quiet powerful authority. In 1990. I was ten years married with two children. This time it was like a volcano. One which I thought was extinct. It was very hot. I had to wear my sunglasses because I was weeping day and night. I wept for months before I knew what it was really about. Externally everything was perfect. I was happily married. The children were fine. Finally, there it was, the calling. As life. That's why I think at that conference I referred to it as a child I had lost or a baby that the authorities had forced me to abort and then it was alive and kicking and would not then be silenced. That was different then. I was thirty-three. Then I said a wholehearted "yes."

When I was back in college the prayer was "do not call me. Your church doesn't want me." A very anguished prayer. I said "yes," I'll leave the working out to God. I suppose I got an inner sense again. It's the work of the Holy Spirit. Without the Holy Spirit there would be none of this.

A: And so, the second time you said "yes," there were your children; there was your husband, you had studied theology. What did you do?

S: It's hard to convey but it was such a powerful experience, inside it was like I was falling apart. I was undone. Something big shifts on the inside and you are hanging on by a tiny thread. It's being done unto you; you just try to surrender to that process and to let it have its way. Then, finally after all those tears, it was so joyful because it was alive. It was alive.

I was so naïve. When one experiences such a powerful breakthrough within oneself, I got a sense that there would be a breakthrough externally too. No doubt that they are going to see the light or see something. I had to tell Colm and try to explain what was going on underneath. Colm took it on board. His wife of ten years. And then I went back to the chaplain whom I had known in Trinity and he said, "Well if it has come back, perhaps there is something more to it than just a passing fad."

I started wondering whether there must be other women, because I couldn't be an exception, and found there were others. There was one, older, woman I who had known since she was a child. I was reading Nóirín ni Rían recently, and she knew from when she was a child. A friend I knew, Delma Sheridan, she's dead now, but she had known since she was young. All these women. You think you're the only one and therefore you are isolated. I have compared it to gay people and this was the same. Gay people are in the closet and it is the same with women with vocations. I was told, "You should be ashamed of yourself, saying you are called. It's wanting power or it's delusion, it's pride or it's because you don't accept being a woman, or you are clericalized and you don't think it's good enough to be a baptized Christian." I said, "No, no. That's not it. That's not it."

Very early on I was interviewed on French television about my sense of vocation. As I sat on the suburban train into Paris I was suddenly overwhelmed by a very dark oppressive feeling and an inner voice saying: "You have no vocation: you are deceiving yourself and you are going to deceive all these people." As I sat there a busker came into my carriage and started singing, but interrupted himself: "I am going to tell you the story of Mary of Nazareth. As she stood at the foot of the cross she said: 'My God, I give him back to you, my flesh and blood.'" That was all. The dark oppressive feeling lifted as instantly as it had come and I was completely freed of doubt. I have never forgotten it.

Well the penny started dropping after a few weeks that there wasn't going to be an announcement in Rome so I realised that I was going to have to do some of the work. I spoke to Donal Murray who was the local bishop and I knew him. You must remember now what for me after all the pain and everything, when finally, the call came, I heard it and said yes to it—it was very joyful.

A: You seem very lit up, actually, talking about it.

S: It was good news to be called. It was good news for me and I thought it was good news for the church, for the world. Then I went to see poor Donal Murray and I was full of this good news. And I realised this was not good news it was a bloody headache! I was full of this enthusiasm and this good news! You're looking for priests, look, God is calling women! And poor Donal was disconcerted, "And how would we know? We could be laying hands on you women and how would we know?" I said, "How do you know about men?" He said, "The sacrament takes…" That was the beginning of realising. To be asked for proof. What kind of proof can you ever offer? Then I met other bishops and intended perhaps to speak to the pope. In '93 I went to meet John Magee because he had been secretary to the pope. I thought the pope can't make any decisions without knowing so I asked had he met any women called to be priests, and John Magee said, "No, not to his knowledge."

Eventually, we started BASIC (Brothers and Sisters in Christ), Colm, myself, and Fr. Eamon McCarthy, who had been chaplain in Trinity. He could see the continuity and that's why we included him. We started off with a petition to end church discrimination against women. Women are baptised, women are confirmed, one baptism, one Spirit, one God, Greek or Jew, slave or free, male or female.[1] People are just called to ministries. The gifts don't come gender-labelled—pink gifts. To open that gift was to give God the freedom to call who God wants. I remember at the time you couldn't have female altar servers either. This was the climate. There was good feedback and a group was started and I met bishops, I met cardinals, I traipsed the length and the breadth and I wrote letters. I tried everything. I went to Krakow in the depths of winter to meet an old friend of John Paul II going back to underground seminary times, thinking perhaps he could pass on a message. I went to Rome seven times and I got nowhere.

I thought, "Perhaps I'll get ready at least." In the early nineties I went to Milltown and did my theology. After that I studied ecumenical

---

1. Citing Paul's Epistle to the Galatians 3:28.

theology. I couldn't go back to this narrow theology which seemed one dimensional. It was still very clericalized and I couldn't breathe so I left after the first year and went on and started BASIC. I didn't know I would start BASIC but that's what came after.

A: So, you tried a campaign?

S: Yes, because I realised there were other women. I knew that those categories that as a child were so drilled into me, that God only calls men to the priesthood, were false. These were so strong that when the call came I remember thinking, "Well am I a man or a woman?' But I knew. What really did affect me was that all those decisions were made without listening to the experience of what God was doing now in the lives of so many women. And we deserve a hearing because any process of discernment to be true its name cannot take place without listening. Otherwise it's lip service to what God is doing. Gradually you get a sense of church authorities cutting off the oxygen.

A: When you say it cuts off the oxygen—has it died?

S: Well there is a deadliness because if you silence the voice of the Spirit through people you cut off the oxygen. You can't breathe or your breathing is so shallow you just have enough. And then your energy is simply spent. I couldn't believe the poor priest, Eamon, who stood by my sense of calling because he saw what it did to me back in college. He ended up out of ministry for five years. This was at a time when priests were abusing children. He was treated like this because he spoke in favour of the ordination of women. He refused to sign the oath—as you know, it became part of the oath—he couldn't sign it and he was never made parish priest to this day.[2] But he was back in ministry after Des Connell left.

There is a distortion at the heart. At one level I could see this was giving me life and opening me up, and then from the other it was like a smothering and being blocked. Gradually, later on, I used the word "crucifixion." I had been crucified. Jesus was crucified also because he had blasphemed, he had made claims.

At the heart of the good news is reconciliation. I find between men and women the church is not an agent of that reconciliation. In a

---

2. Office holders in the Catholic Church are required to sign an oath to uphold the faith of the church. In 1998, this specifically included a commitment to the church position on the ordination of women.

world where there is so much sexism, including spiritually, sadly the church is a counter-witness. It gives a distorted image of God. It's a male God ultimately. Yes, women are in the image of God, but not as much as the man is. Christ is the image of God, the Father/Mother, so then in whose image are we? Our bodies are deemed unworthy. I said that to Diarmuid Martin, "Well, we are not redeemed, because what has not been assumed in the incarnation is not redeemed." I said, "We have an inclusive theology of creation and incarnation and redemption, but then your theology of priesthood contradicts it."

To me it has done great damage to the church. The church is never for itself, the church is for the world, but sadly it contributes to the abuse of women. And where women, where anybody, is abused, God is abused. What you do to the least of my brothers and sisters, you do to me. Discrimination is done to the Christ, and maybe done in the name of Christ but is done "unto me." I call it a form of spiritual abuse.

A: Did you continue to minister in various ways or did you focus on campaigning and speaking?

S: With BASIC I was the visible person because a lot of women said that they couldn't afford to do it. I had also left the marriage counselling. If you're very prominent with something like that you're not going to be invited to anything. Others were in ministry; were religious; were lecturing or chaplaincy or whatever and they couldn't afford to speak. So, it was painful to realise, because I was still quite young then, that that would be the price to pay. But I did a lot with BASIC and part of it was listening to other women's pain, their journey. There was writing and there was the international dimension.

I started presiding at the Eucharist. Bishop Larry Ryan was bishop of Carlow. He said, "Why do you want to be a priest?" I said, "Actually I didn't want." I said, "If it disturbs you it disturbed me first!" He asked and I said, "I don't know, I didn't call myself!" But certainly, I didn't want to preside. I was afraid it would be an ego trip. That I would be grasping at something. To me the Eucharist is the very opposite. It is self-giving, as Jesus left it to us, not grasping. Then eventually it came from something unplanned.

It was just after the conference in '95. I got into an inner black pit, just after Christmas. I found there was a live butterfly under the Christmas tree. I associate the butterfly with resurrection: coming out of the disintegration in the chrysalis and then new life. I got the sense, now is the time to celebrate Eucharist. I said, "Okay God, you can ask me anything you want, you're God so you are entitled to ask me, but I would want to see that it is you, and that it is not my delusion or that I am doing it." I was very afraid to be egotistical. I was still praying about it and I didn't want to rush.

A few days later a friend, a missionary sister, who knew I had a sense of vocation to the priesthood visited me. She said, "Soline, I don't know why but when I was in France this summer, I bought a chalice and a paten, and I brought them back to Africa and was going to give them to a priest. For some reason I didn't. I got a sense to bring them back and give them to you now." And she said, "The gestation has been long and it doesn't look like Rome is ready but your time has come." And she gave me this chalice. I said, "You know what, I had asked for a sign, because I had said it would be nice to get a little sign that I'm not making it up."

It all unfolded on the feast of the Epiphany. I presided at the Eucharist at the table there, and there were three men. Three wise men! My friend the religious sister couldn't come. One of the lovely things that happened was that I went and got a bottle of wine from our garage, and I pulled it at random. I don't know how we got it or where—Chateau St. Marie!—Mary's wine! Very joyful. Gosh, I can tell you, the trepidation. It reminded me of giving birth. The lovely thing is that when you've given birth you know that it comes from you. You know you're not faking it. It comes from deep within you. And when I was there it was like the first, you hardly know how to hold . . . but at the same time, you know that you're not pretending, you're not "playing at" being mother. You see when you hold your newborn you know it's true. It was the same for me with celebrating the Eucharist. The first time, my friend, a priest, had to tell me the rubrics, every movement, but there was that lovely sense. That's why for me, it's obviously not giving birth physically, but it's a lovely experience when like a new mother, you don't quite know what to do, but you know it's you. You're not pretending; you're not faking it. What I'm trying to convey is there was a sense of yes, it's who I am, it's who God has made me. I am not being an imposter. Presiding at Eucharist ranked as a grave crime against the faith deserving excommunication. It's ranked with, which was very hurtful when it was reaffirmed, it's ranked in the same category as sexual abuse.

A: and no one has been excommunicated as a result of that.

S: They are not excommunicated.

A: So that was a big step?

S: You see, everything I have tried to do has been a response. I have not taken the initiative. I have made mistakes. I am trying to respond as faithfully as I can. Now I am not one hundred percent faithful all the time, but I can say honestly that that is my deepest desire, to respond faithfully to God's presence and God's action. Ultimately, it's love responding to love. Do you remember I said that before all of that was an experience of a profound experience of God's love for me, and for the whole world? I wasn't an exception. That is the whole Trinitarian message to me, that communion of love, and I am responding to being called into that. So, it's a response to that impulse which lives at the heart of creation.

The heart of my vocation is to understand that every human being is invited to respond to that powerful life-giving energy we call love. Priesthood is part of that context. That is the form that it has taken for me, but it can take any form and not one bigger or better than the other. I see people trying to respond to their vocation but it's responding to what the Spirit is doing in them.

There was another poor bishop, at the end, he said, "Perhaps one of your sons will have your vocation." Even the logic—*your* vocation, not even *a* vocation to priesthood. I called him back for a meeting and said, "Do you realise what you said there? I might as well be dead. If it is my vocation and my son is expected to live it." I said, "I will not put the burden of my unfulfilled vocation on my son." After that meeting I thought I might as well be dead. At one level he heard which is more than others did. And he felt obviously there was a genuine vocation because he said "your vocation," but then obviously the head says, "No because . . ." and if he had listened he probably wouldn't be a bishop now.

So, in this way we continue as before. We don't have to make any changes; we don't have to grasp any nettles; ruffle any feathers; look again at our theology and say, "Where did we start going wrong?" You know, you have stuff in your attic or your garage and you say, "Why am I keeping that? It's no longer of use." Or "it was working but now it has perished." And in the church we need a lot of spring cleaning.

A: So, what should happen? Obviously you want things to change for women in ministry.

S: I think God wants! That's a great thing. I think the older you get the bolder you are!

A: And how would you see change coming?

S: It's changing in all kinds of ways. It's like sprouting, you know? I met the nuncio a long time ago, Emmanuel Gerada. A very sad man underneath. I asked, "Why are my letters to the pope not answered?" He said, "The pope doesn't meet people like you. The pope meets cardinals." You know, this big bubble of power; this illusion of control. You know what? God is in charge. Change is happening. Whether God is allowed or not, God is in charge. God could still reach me and countless other women also, so change is happening in millions of ways. It's like me, if I thought I could stop all the weeds growing in my garden, but there are all those weeds growing—people weeds!

A: In the questionnaire I asked, "If you are not ordained, do you feel a call to ordination?" All the Catholic women said "no." Many of them added, "I used to feel a call to ordination but now the system is so bad or toxic I wouldn't go near it." What would be your response to that?

S: I never felt called to the clerical, the clericalization of the ministry. I never saw myself wearing a Roman collar. I was already so ecumenical. I was already in college attending daily Mass except on Wednesdays when I would go to the Church of Ireland Communion service, so I wouldn't fit in that model.

A: Your priesthood doesn't reflect the clericalized model?

S: A lot of men are also limited by this model. I go back to the gospel and the person of Christ, I go back to the Spirit, I go back to love. There is no love without freedom. One has to query why many of our priests are so trapped. You don't get that sense of freedom. They'll tell you, "I can't say that, or I'm afraid to this or that." The saddest thing is, "keep your head below the parapet," and having to say things that don't come from the heart. So how can you minister? Who would want to be that? Jesus was free, and that was part of the attraction. He was free and then he could free people.

It has been a journey of discovery but I don't have any illusions left. Ultimately, they are themselves abused and they abuse in turn. I hate to say that abuse gets passed down the whole hierarchical chain of command. You crush the people below you and in turn they crush others, since they have been crushed. Since they have silenced their conscience to obey, they expect you do to the same. This is what the bishop said to Eamonn McCarthy, "Well I obey, you obey me."

A: Is there any hope?

S: There's always hope. Where there's God there's hope. The theology of hope was my thesis. We live in joyful hope. It used to be in the prayer of the Eucharist. Joyful hope.

Pat Storey

Maynooth, 2017

BISHOP PAT STOREY GREW up in Belfast. She studied French and English at Trinity College Dublin. She was ordained deacon in the Church of Ireland in 1997 and priest in 1998. She served her curacy in the Parish of Kilconriola and Ballyclug, Ballymena, and then served at St. Aidan's Church, Glenavy, County Antrim. In 2004, she was appointed rector of St. Augustine's Church in Derry. She was appointed bishop of the United Dioceses of Meath and Kildare in September 2013. Pat is married to Earl and they have two adult children. She enjoys walking, reading, and creative writing.

A: What drew you into ministry?

P: I was brought up in a completely secular environment and when I went to university in Trinity College Dublin, the only person I knew going from my school was somebody who was a very committed Christian. And I remember thinking, "Oh no, this is going to cramp my style." But, just being with her actually really worked on me. She talked about her faith a lot and it was obviously very important to her. I suppose eventually I began to think I might be missing out on something. I began to read the gospels and that was what changed my life. I suppose I thought, "I like this person of Jesus. He really stands out to me. I really like what he stands for. I like his values and his approach to people."

I was nineteen and I made a commitment of faith. Almost immediately I'd say I felt a call to Christian leadership but I didn't know what form that would take. So that was a long time coming, it was years and years. My husband was ordained and I used to watch him and think, "I think I could do that," but the church wasn't ordaining women at that point so it just wasn't an issue. Then when the children were small and the church was ordaining women I gradually began to think about it. I do remember a light bulb moment, when I was at theological college and somebody said there's a couple in theological college training for ministry who are engaged. I thought, "Oh so a couple can do this." My poor husband was appalled at the thought of two people in ministry, not because it was me, or because he had any problem with women in ministry, but he just thought, "Oh my goodness, two of us doing this, are you joking?" So, we had a bit of to-ing and fro-ing between us for quite a long time before he said, "Look you've just got to push the doors and see if they open," and they did.

It was very gradual in one way and yet very clearly a light bulb moment in another way when I thought, "I have to do this. Or at least I have to push the doors." I would say it started, with personal faith, and then the feeling that I was drawn to Christian leadership of some kind, and then ordination came into the picture. But that was between 1978 and 1997 when I was ordained, so that was a long, long time for it to work on me. Marriage and kids took up a lot of my time and thought for a long time. Even when I went into training my kids were seven and three. I don't necessarily recommend that everybody goes into full-time theological training when their children are that young, but I just knew I had to do it. I had a very strong call on my life.

A: You've used that phrase once or twice now, "I had to, felt compelled." Can you say more about that?

P: Well my husband would say that too. He felt that this train was leaving the station whether I was on it or not. I had a really strong sense that this was my life's purpose; that this was for me. I hadn't been involved in women's push for ordination or anything like that. It really was entirely separate and entirely private. I remember there was about a year when the children were small when I went off to the mountains in Wicklow to really think and pray because I thought, "I need to be sure about this," you know, "it's a big change for even us as a family and as a couple." So, I spent a long time, and we spent a long time as a couple thinking and praying about it. Then Earl said, and I felt as well, that once that moment happened the train was leaving the station. It was a very sudden and very strong call.

A: It seems the primary issue was your marriage. How did that play out?

P: Well it was the marriage and the family. I would say that the young children were a factor because I knew that that would be difficult. I also knew that at that point in my life I wanted to do something more. I was a full-time mum. I'd been at home for seven years, and Luke was only three. I loved being a mum, but there's more that I needed to do. I would still say that being a full-time mum was the hardest job I ever did in my entire life. I watch my daughter do it and I couldn't go back there. We knew it would be difficult because it's weekends and evenings as well as days. When you've small children that's babysitters and working out what nights are we out this week. So, to some extent my husband was right in his reservations and as it was a very difficult dynamic, which is known to many professional couples. When I had to throw commuting into the mix, that really nearly put me over the edge. The commute was about thirty miles but it meant going over and coming back for tea and going back for an evening meeting, so I did that journey at least four times a day. It was never about the spiritual or about the call, it was just about how on earth do we work this out as a couple with young children? I would say it nearly took us ten years to work that through.

      Then we worked together for two or three years. That brought different challenges! We wanted to stay married! Then Earl decided—he'd been in ministry twenty years—that he would do something different. At that time, I stepped into being a rector in Derry, so we almost took it in turns to take a rector's role in parish ministry. We never really wanted to be two different rectors in two different communities.

A: I suppose that in the church there weren't a lot of people already doing it.

P: Well I think I was in the second batch of pioneers because there were quite a few women ordained when it was first brought in, and some would have been in clergy couples. That raised issues for them in that I remember the first women who were part of an ordained couple were nearly placed a couple of hundred miles apart for curacies. I just knew that couldn't work for us. I don't think the church knew what to do with ordained couples and to some extent I'm not sure they still do and it's not ideal but if you know it's right for you, you just have to work it through. But look, we did it and we got there and we're still together and we love each other so we're very lucky.

A: Congratulations!

P: Thank you. I feel that that deserves a medal, especially for him!

A: You've had to move around a good bit by the sound of things.

P: Yes. When I started training Earl was in Shankhill and Bray, and then when I was in my final year he moved to a job in Belfast which gave me the chance to be a curate in Ballymena. And then when I was in my final year of that he went back to Glenavy in County Antrim and I had to start commuting, and after that I went to Derry. And after Derry I came here. The kids were at different schools. That wasn't easy although they look back on that and feel that it really gave them skills in terms of meeting new people and being independent. There were lots of downsides but there were plus sides in that they're very good at going into a room and going over to somebody and introducing themselves and not waiting for somebody else to come to them, because they had to do that to survive.

A: Over that period of twenty years, do you see changes for women? Has it changed?

P: It has changed in that it's become the new normal. Although I would have to be honest and say I still think that when somebody is choosing their new rector that they always think about women when they've run out of male names. I think there is equality, but in people's heads, the vicar's still a man. Maybe we have to think afresh.

A: So, the woman vicar?

P: Yes, it has become the new normal, particularly in the south. There are a lot more women in ministry in the south than in Northern Ireland and there are more rectors. I find a lot of women, and I don't blame them at all because I considered the same thing, think it's easier to go non-stipendiary which means that they don't have to think about taking responsibility for a parish and being placed or moved, but that they can function and raise a family and it is easier. I think women are about twenty percent of clergy and not all of those would be full time. People don't blink now when they see a woman in a clerical collar but I do think still when parishes are choosing their clergy they don't automatically think of a woman.

A: Do women find it harder to get a placement?

P: I think that's probably still true. I didn't have people queuing out the door before I went to Derry. It's not meant to be discriminatory but it's a hangover from the past and a result of ninety percent of vicars being male, so nine times out of ten you're right!

A: Has being a woman influenced your ministry?

P: I never know how to answer that question. I think I bring being a woman to ministry, with all that that means, and you can't really generalise about men and women too much. Sometimes these things are about temperament rather than gender. I do think that, in general, women make decisions in a different way, in that I feel that I am more collegial and collaborative than some men. But I know lots of men that are collegial and lots of women that aren't. I would say that my way of making decisions comes from a huge desire to bring people along with me so I wouldn't be authoritarian or it wouldn't be "this is what we're doing, jump on board." I have a senior team here where we make decisions together. I wouldn't be afraid of saying, "No I don't agree with that, I'm not going down that road," but it's a less authoritarian approach to leadership.

I just bring being feminine to the job. Women would probably say that they find it easy to talk to me because I'm another female. I'm a mother. I understand what it's like to have a teenager or a small baby. I've just become a granny so that's very exciting. I know what it is to become be a granny, so obviously men know what it is to be a dad and a granddad and that sort of thing, but it is different when you meet someone in church leadership who's a mother. It's a difficult question to answer without generalising and I'm quite an extrovert and quite assertive so I'm probably behave very like a man in some contexts, or as people would see behaving like a man, so it's a difficult one to answer.

A: Have there been defining moments in your ministry?

P: Well the obvious moment which was defining was when I was phoned to say I'd been elected the bishop of Meath and Kildare. And alongside being the first female bishop, for me it was just being a bishop. I had never considered it. I didn't even know what a bishop did. One of the really helpful things that day was the archbishop of Armagh who rang about the job said, "Trust the church, and trust the process." That was so helpful because I couldn't say I felt a strong call to be a bishop, because I didn't and it was out of the blue. I had to trust that others had discerned that process and that somehow the Holy Spirit was working in that process. For me it was a shock and I had to trust others this it was correct because it was months before I worked it out for myself that it was correct.

A: How does that happen?

P: In the Church of Ireland every diocese has an election board made up of people from their own diocese but also people from others. If that college fails to elect with a certain majority the decision goes to the House of Bishops, which happened in my case. If the decision goes to the House of Bishops that can literally be anybody. There are no applications; no nominations; no interview, you're just elected, and that's what happened in my case, which is probably why it was a complete shock. And normally that decision would be to somebody who had climbed the seniority ladder which I hadn't. I hadn't been a canon or a dean or an archdeacon or progressed in any of the normal ways.

A: That's quite unusual then?

P: It is quite unusual, so it was a big jump, and very daunting indeed. I remember that first day when the news broke, it was big news because it was the first woman. I remember having six interviews lined up in a row over the next hour and thinking, "I can't—I just don't think I can do this." My husband runs his own business in PR and communications, so that was very helpful. He really helped and managed me through that day, but it was utterly bewildering.

I got a phone call at five o'clock on Thursday, 19 September. I asked for time to think about it. Apparently, I was the first person to ask for time. I reckon that's a woman thing. I wanted to consult with my family before saying "yes." Whereas I think others had said yes and then consulted. They wanted to know there and then because the media were waiting for news, and I said "no, I need time," so I made the decision at 11 o'clock the next morning.

A: What went through your mind between five o'clock on the Thursday and making the decision?

P: It was a very difficult twenty-four hours. We didn't sleep much. We walked the dog along the Foyle Bridge that night, just talking it over. My husband was on board immediately. He said, "You have to do this, it's a great opportunity. Why would you turn this down?" But I was thinking, "I have to leave my children behind. We have to move again. I don't know Meath and Kildare. It's a long time since we've lived in the Republic. Do I really want to be a bishop? Do I really know what that involves?" All sorts of things. In the end, it was a big risk of faith and trusting the church that they knew better than I did. So, yes, it was a very bewildering forty-eight hours. I would love to live that again where I could actually enjoy the moment, which I can't say I did, but I did really enjoy my consecration.

I just remember I'd settled down so I'd got used to the idea that it was happening. I had thought about me being a bishop, but I hadn't personally thought about the historic moment that it was for the church. I remember just after I was consecrated in the service, you turn around and the archbishop introduces you to the congregation. And the congregation applaud, and the applause went on and on and on and on. I remember thinking, "Oh my goodness. This is actually historic." That was the first time it had occurred to me. There had been a lot of media interest and I knew that I was the first woman but I hadn't really thought about how historic this was for the church until that moment. I just was able to really enjoy that service and I really prayed. Some people asked me, "What will I pray for?" and I said, "Pray that I'll enjoy it; that I won't be so nervous that I feel sick and I just want it over with, a bit like a wedding." You know, you're just so nervous. And I wasn't at all. I was very calm. I felt such a sense of privilege.

I had imposter syndrome for the first year, where I thought, "Why on earth is this happening to me?" but I think that's normal. I worked that through and then the second year, when you're doing everything the second time, things are a lot easier. Yes, it was a definitely sink or swim that first year. There's not much of an induction process. You're fired in and you find your way. I have a huge sense of privilege. I cannot believe that God has given me this wonderful life, and a wonderful opportunity. I feel very blessed. There are down days, of course, it's a normal job. There are days when I feel very stressed because there are big decisions to be made or big problems to face, but in general I feel extremely privileged and blessed to be doing it. I love the doors that it opens. You know that I would never ever get the chance to speak at or be at events unless I was in this role. I'm doing a *Women in Leadership* seminar tomorrow and nobody would have asked me to do that before this appointment. And I love being invited. I get invited quite a lot to solemn novenas in Catholic parishes and I love that, it's one of my favourite things.

A: What do you like about it?

P: I just love the fact that women can see that women can do this. You know a lot of Catholic women come up to me afterwards and say, "It's wonderful to see a woman." I know that they can't in the Catholic Church as yet but it's good for Catholic women to see there is light at the end of the tunnel.

A: And what would you say to people who say that the ordination of women is an obstacle to ecumenism?

P: Well I would say that there have been lots of things through history that have been obstacles to ecumenism and we've got over them all. And there'll be lots of things in the future that could be obstacles to ecumenism. Not every priest or bishop in the Catholic Church feels the same about this. There are lots of priests and bishops who want this to happen, and who want married priests to happen. I really respect the patience that Catholic people have in waiting for this to come about it, and I'm sure it will at some stage. Obviously, I'm not in the know about that but I think there are a lot of people in the hierarchy who are waiting patiently or not so patiently for this to happen. I know when I'm invited to speak it is with an openness, and there is such openness. I suppose that the more women do this job, the more people see that actually it is no big deal. In fact, you bring the yin and the yang. Fifty-two percent of the population is represented when I'm ordained. Yes, it could be an obstacle, but it's not an obstacle for a lot of people, it's actually something that they would really want to see. You know the church is changing. It's changing slowly but it is changing.

A: Are there challenges you face that a man in the same position may not have faced?

P: I don't think so, or discrimination. I have to tell the truth for me. I know that there are women who have, but I feel I've been very fortunate in that I don't feel that my experience in this job is any different from my eleven male colleagues. I suppose you'd have to ask other people whether they experience something different in me being a female, and that might be very useful. I don't know the answer to that because I've never asked. I'd love to ask my eleven colleagues is it different having a woman around the table, because I don't know. I suspect it must be but I'm not really sure how.

A: What was your first meeting with the other bishops like?

P: Well I was so intimidated I just can't remember. Not by eleven men but by the role that I was now playing and my first meeting at this level, so I don't think I said very much—unusual for me they would tell you now. The first few months I was really finding my feet, so but I've never felt treated any differently by any of them. I don't feel treated any differently by this diocese. I am not somebody who seeks offence either. There may have been intentional offence that I didn't pick up which is fine, but I don't look for it. I just get on with my job.

A: Would you like another female bishop?

P: Yes, it would be lovely, and do you know why? Because all they talk about in down time is football, and I would love a woman to sit beside me and talk about something I am actually interested in. My experience around the table is, "Oh please can we talk about something other than sport?" That's because we have dinner together and if we're away on a residential we'll have down time together. I think, "Oh, I wish there was another woman here that we could talk about things that interest women."

A: What do women in ministry need?

P: Women in general are very relational and very community-focussed and so I need people to bounce things off. I have a personal coach which I have found invaluable, in being able to talk things through. I have a husband, I have a great archdeacon and a great PA whom I talk things through with. I now have a senior leadership team of eight where we make decisions together.

The first year was much more difficult because I felt more on my own, whereas the second and third year I feel we're more of a team, leading the diocese. There are lots of challenges into the future in terms of church life and faith. I'm not somebody who functions well alone. I love being on my own. The older I get I think I need, I really need solitude, because I am an extrovert, but in terms of doing the job and making decisions I need a team around me. What do women need? I can only speak for one, and I need a team.

A: You're avoiding generalisations.

P: And yet you kind of have to because to say anything you have to generalise so I'm aware when I say, "Women are more relational or women are more collegial," there might be men sitting there saying well, "No they're not." But I think they are. It's definitely relationships define women much more than they define men I think. I'm sure somebody will shake me down for that. That's okay. Let them!

A: Any hopes for the future?

P: I am one of twelve which means the percentage of women in senior leadership in the church is low, so I'd love to see more. I'm not particularly in favour of positive discrimination so I really hope that I got the job on my own merits, and I would hope that any other woman got the job on their own merit. I think that otherwise it's insulting. I want to be chosen for Pat and not for, "gosh we'd better get a woman in." I really want it to be the right person. I do understand that sometimes in institutions in particular that there has to be some sort of bias towards women, but I would prefer that a woman gets elected on their own merit. I'd like it to be more than one in twelve in terms of senior leadership. Gradually women are in senior positions throughout the church in terms of deans, and archdeacons and that's all happening. And because there are only twelve of us the positions come up very irregularly.

When I went into it, it was just so difficult to go into full-time ministry with a young family. I don't know what the solutions to that are, but women do take the easier route which is the non-stipendiary, because it will have less impact on family life. That goes for other professions too. A lot of women take part-time teaching and job shares and for exactly the same reasons. There are extra difficulties with our working hours, because they're unsocial hours so I think it is more difficult to go into full-time ministry.

A: And do they have less influence in non-stipendiary ministry?

P: I think so. No matter how you look at it, if you're full-time in a position and you're full-time salaried or you're part time and you're non salaried, there is a difference. Whether we like it or not; or whether that should be the case or not, the amount of influence is definitely different, which is why I didn't want to do that. It's all happening under the radar. If you look at the church now as opposed to ten years ago there are many more women in senior positions. It's just that these opportunities don't come along very often, because we're a small church.

A: I understand that there used to be a group for women who were ordained and that after a certain point they preferred to discontinue?

P: That group was needed for a while to get the ordination of women through, but I never wanted to be in a women's group or a women's ministry group because I just felt I wanted to be a minister or a priest or a curate or whatever I was. I always wanted men and women to work together. I still just want to be a bishop, I don't want to be a woman bishop, but you have to live in the real world. I get that it's a big thing for others, but I suppose the gender issue isn't a huge thing for me. I feel like I'm a Church of Ireland bishop. I happen to be a woman. I do recognise of course that I'm the first and the only one at present. On one level it's a big deal and on another level for me it isn't.

Conclusion

"Called . . ."

IRELAND HAS SEEN THE Christian ministry of women for over fifteen hundred years. During this time some have become known, remarkable amid the processions of ministering men. Brigid, Nano Nagle, Alice Cambridge, Catherine McAuley, Charlotte Pym, Catherine Reynolds, Mary Aikenhead, Betty Barclay, Barbara Blagdon, Ruth Patterson, Kathleen Young, Irene Templeton, Ginnie Kennerley, Ellen Whalley, Stanislaus Kennedy, Carol Barry, Heather Morris, Pat Storey, Soline Humbert, Julie Kavanagh, and Margaret Kiely are some visible examples of the thousands of women who have responded to God's call to a life of ministry on this island, and also sent from its shores.

The women who participated in this study feel blessed in responding to God's call on their lives. They feel privileged to care for people at times of joy and sorrow; to preach the gospel; lead the church; work for justice and accompany others in spiritual growth. They love being bishop, chaplains, priests, youth ministers, theologians, diocesan leaders, social reformers, deaconesses, educators and religious sisters. They love being mums, wives, grandmas, friends, and neighbours. They love a good laugh. They love to pray. They love God.

The women who participated in this study do not wish to be set apart but to minister to God's people unencumbered. They expressed the desire not to be a "breath of fresh air," or better or more holy than their brother ministers, but to serve in ministry and deal with the daily challenges it brings. However, it is the ministry of women which is seen as contentious, or transgressive. Male ministers do not have to contend with questioning from family, friends, or church people about the propriety of their ministry. They do not have to attend a theological college where they feel merely tolerated. They do not have to do their ministry learning in their first post with the added burden of representing the success or failure of their gender. They do not have to deal with people's sexism, "banter," inappropriate touching or expectation that they will flirt with them. They do not have to see the jobs in theology, preaching, finance, and leadership go to others on the basis of gender and not talent. They do not have listen to rumours in their church that their ordination is invalid or should be discontinued. They do not have feel that they should speak or act in resistance to gender injustice and then be seen as disloyal for doing so. They do not have to choose between their calling and earning a wage to raise their families. They do not have to twist and turn themselves in order to fit in to a model which at best was not designed for them and at worst conspires to exclude them. They do not have to feel second best; there on sufferance, or to decide that they will choose to say one thing at the meeting because their colleagues will not tolerate two. Many, many women do.

In this study women whose nature and roles have been much discussed by others have spoken for themselves. The primary research question, *What is your experience as a female minister at this time?* has uncovered a tradition which has been scantily traced in the past—that of women ministering in the Christian church.

SUMMARY OF FINDINGS

Women in ministry in Ireland are dedicated to their service to God's people and their churches. Call is an overarching presence in everything they do and is the source of their motivation and nourishment. They frame their commentary in terms of their faith and their sense of mission and church.

The view of the great majority is that the gendering of ministry is unnecessary and detrimental to the participation of women. Participants wish to promote diverse gifts in ministry and to play an equal part in this. They acknowledge that they are working in environments which have largely evolved to serve a system with men at its centre and which often does not serve women's participation. They would like to see new models for ministry. They would like to reimagine the role of spouses and children of ministers and see creative responses to their needs during the especially demanding years of young families.

These ministers do not have any doubts about their calling and role and are willing to accommodate and work with those who have genuine theological concerns about women in ministry. They are notably lacking in ambition for personal career development within church structures and hierarchies, and are slow to trust church power structures. Those who are ordained and in leadership positions still feel that they are constantly evaluated because they are among the first or are in a minority as female ministers.

Most in the Catholic Church do not wish to be ordained in the current dispensation. They wish to see changes in a system they deem to be impoverished and outmoded for clergy and laity, women and men, alike. They most need to have fair and life-giving foundations for their ministries including ongoing formation and fair remuneration and conditions. They wish to reach their full potential and calling in appropriate ministerial contexts. Most support the ordination of women in principle.

Women in the Church of Ireland, the Methodist Church in Ireland, and some smaller Protestant denominations appreciate the commitment to equality within these denominations and express their hope that this will continue to grow. While not perfect, most see their churches as places where women can flourish in ministry. Participants from the Presbyterian Church in Ireland also feel that their church has supported their ministry despite the misgivings of some colleagues. They hope that it will continue to uphold the equal status of women in ministry.

Participants expressed a desire for greater ecumenical cooperation and for their sisters across the traditions to flourish. Many expressed concern for Catholic women. At the research gathering some expressed surprise that Catholic women were involved in so many ministries. Many expressed a desire for solidarity among women across the denominations and opportunities to work, reflect and pray together.

QUESTIONS FOR FURTHER EXPLORATION

The delicate and sometimes vexed issue of women's ministry can only be addressed in churches with the full participation of female church members, ministers, and theologians. This study indicates that three areas are most pressing. These are the questions of gender and power; ministry and vocation; and ecumenism.

Gender and Power

What kinds of power are appropriate in the Christian community and its structures and ministries? What characterises the models of power currently operating in churches? What kind of conversion needs to take place so that models of power in our churches reflect the values and theologies we claim to espouse? If the models of power in the church are ensuring that men have more power than women, and in fact great power over women, how has this been justified and legitimised theologically?

Where women in this study comment on power they expressed their belief that the power structures in churches do not reflect the power exemplified by Jesus in the gospel, and they feel they particularly suit a "male model."

Churches espouse the idea of gender equality but, while women experience elements of this, it is not fully achieved. Mary McAleese asked the Catholic hierarchy what they were doing to promote women's participation in the church in the absence of women's ordination, saying that the permanent exclusion of women from priesthood had

> locked women out of any significant role in the church's leadership and authority structure. Yet in justice their very permanent exclusion from priesthood should have provoked the church to find innovative ways of including women's voices as of right in the divinely instituted College of Bishops and the man-made entities such as the College of Cardinals, the Synod of Bishops and episcopal conferences. Just imagine the normative scenario: Pope Francis calls a Synod on Women and 350 male celibates advise the Pope on what women really want. That is how ludicrous our church has become. How long can the hierarchy sustain the credibility of a God who wants things this way, who wants a church where women and are invisible and voiceless in leadership and decision-making?[1]

If churches wish to theologise about women being equal but different, it is incumbent upon them to show an unequivocal commitment to this equality in their structures. Dr. McAleese goes on:

> The Catholic Church has long since been a primary global carrier of the virus of misogyny. It has never sought a cure though a cure is freely available. Its name is "equality."

---

1. McAleese, "The Time Is Now."

Her point is made in the Catholic context but is relevant to other churches. Unless churches of all hues are committed to the equal treatment of women, they will perpetuate power structures which are sinful by their own definitions.

This further creates the question of whether the failure to promote the full participation of women also perpetrates an injustice against men, boys and the churches. If abundant life promised by Jesus is the mark of the reign of God (John 10:10b), and it is prevented in the church community, this failure prevents the experience of the reign of God among the whole community.

The churches must ask themselves whether they believe in the equality of women and men, of girls and boys in the sight of God. If they wish to say that they do, this has to be seen in practical ecclesial reframing which actively promotes the flourishing of women and their full contribution. This can be measured and evaluated in church structures, policies, opportunities, and budgets.

Ministry and Vocation

Participants of this study proposed that they had inherited a "male model of ministry," which raises the question of whether it is appropriate that models of ministry are gendered? We have seen that historically models of ministry have been gendered just by the assumption that men would be ministers, as were many other models of professions. Should this still be the case for ministry?

Responders characterised a "male" model of ministry as isolated and authoritarian rather than relational and collaborative. In the associated clerical model, the ordained male is seen as subject and this can objectify others who are defined by their relation to him. The lay person, the clergy wife, and the congregation are caught up in a system which prioritises and centralises the role and person of the minister, inhibiting the flourishing of other church members.

In this model, where the priest is theologian he claims more authority; where he is chaplain he is assumed to have gifts that others do not, and so on. While theologised in terms of service, ordination is seen to endow men with multiple advantages which make them more valuable than others before God and the church.[2] If women had always been admitted to all

2. The Catholic Rite of Ordination to the Priesthood uses the word "servant,"

ministries, clericalism may still have been present but not gendered, but we shall never know. As it is, clericalism operates as part of a "male model," and contributes to the sense that women express of not fitting the mould. In the Catholic tradition, where only men can be ordained, this is particularly prevalent and provides a significant impediment to the flourishing of women in ministry.

In this study, insofar as alternative models were proposed, they were characterised by values of collaboration and mutuality. If women are bringing new or different qualities to ministry which are not part of the "male-only" model, how do these characteristics integrate with Christian tradition and theology? Two areas particularly emerge here.

The first is the interpretation of call. Women who have had a relatively smooth passage believe that this confirms their call—that God has opened the doors. How then can women interpret it when the path to their ministry is blocked? Further attention should be given to how the call to ministry is discerned by individuals and churches. Is discernment dependent on existing permissions, that is, is God perceived as unable or prevented from calling women, suitable in all other ways, based on their gender? By what criteria do the churches recognise an authentic call to ministry and are they fit for purpose? How do theologies of discernment which apply in other areas of spiritual and church life apply to women who are discerning a vocation to ministry?[3]

Responders drew the distinction between being called and sent. Are there women in churches who have experienced the authentic call of God but whom the churches refuse to send? What does it mean for God to call a woman in a church which does not recognise this call? The distinction between being called and sent lays the burden of responsibility on the ecclesial community to discern God's action. Whose voice is heard in this process and whose voices are excluded? Where is there continuity with tradition and where is the continuity incomplete or ruptured?

How should ministers be supported in practice? Many research participants seek and organise their own pastoral care and support. However, there is a responsibility of churches also to support their ministers. When a woman follows a vocation, she should be assured of fair treatment, spiritual support, and a reasonable standard of living. The stories of "real poverty"

---

throughout, fourteen times in all.

3. Here I am thinking of the prioritisation of conscience and personal guidance by the Holy Spirit, which are commonly affirmed by churches.

and isolation shared by some of the Catholic women in this study in particular are not only a private concern but an ecclesial one.

The findings of this study raise many questions about flourishing in Christian ministry. These can only be fully addressed by a longitudinal study with diverse ministers.[4] One of many fruits of this may be insights into whether ministry is experienced differently by women and men and how women and men can be supported in their roles.

Ecumenism

The findings of this research demonstrate a shared and common experience of ministry regardless of the particularities of denomination or geography, though these have an influence. This indicates that theologies of ministry may be explored ecumenically. Hitherto these explorations have focussed on differences in theological understandings of ordination, succession and sacrament. This study indicates the probability that cooperative approaches may yield better ecumenical fruit.

The ordination of women has been identified by some, particularly in the Catholic and Orthodox Churches, as a potential obstacle to Christian unity. After the Church of England Synod voted to admit women to the episcopacy in 2008, Cardinal Walter Kasper addressed the Lambeth conference describing the effect of this decision, which

> effectively and definitively blocks a possible recognition of Anglican orders by the Catholic Church.[5]

As we have seen, asked whether they believed the ordination of women to be an obstacle to ecumenical relations, Pat Storey and Heather Morris said they did not, and shared the view that other problems have been overcome and that it would be possible to overcome this one too. No participant expressed concerns about differences in ecclesial understandings of ordination. This supports the view that practical and inductive approaches to the issue of ministry may be life-giving for church dialogue.

4. The Living Ministry study currently underway in the Church of England is a good example of such a study.

5. Kasper, August 2008, cited by Zagano *Women & Catholicism*, 113. This Anglican decision led to the formation of the Personal Ordinariate of Our Lady of Walsingham in 2011 by Pope Benedict XVI to "allow Anglicans to enter into the full communion of the Catholic Church whilst retaining much of their heritage and traditions. It now has the full support and blessing of Pope Francis" (111).

As has been indicated, there is also a question about the diminishing effect on the wider church where the full participation and flourishing of women is not encouraged. As well as seeing the ordination of women in some churches as an obstacle to communion with other churches, ecumenical dialogue should focus on the potential loss or disfigurement to the church when women are not fully admitted to ministries in the churches.

Participants and responders felt that greater ecumenical cooperation would be beneficial to all churches in reflecting on ministerial formation and ongoing support of those in ministry. Findings also reflect a desire among women to experience solidarity and support in ministry across the churches. It is reported across this study that the ministry of women in sister churches encourages women in all churches. While change may be slow and difficult the ecumenical solidarity of women can both ease the struggle and help to achieve progress.

PERSONAL REFLECTION

I feel grateful for the privilege of meeting women in ministry and curating their voices in this work. I have been entrusted with their very personal experiences of God's call; their journey to ministry; their hopes and disappointments; their spiritual life and the joys and challenges of their day to day ministries and the other aspects of their lives. In each woman's reflections there is a unique expression of discipleship and ministry. There is a unique expression of the fruitfulness of a particular relationship between God and a faithful person.

These ministers are kind and gracious. They responded with thought and good humour to my questions. They are humble and uncomplaining; prayerful, sincere, and gifted. They see the church as it is with all its problems and speak constructively about growth and reform—the "truth in love" (Eph 4:15).

A vision for church emerges from this experience which comes from a great diversity of people but is remarkably coherent. These women demonstrate that the endeavour of church can be successful. They speak about the joy of the gospel; collaboration; inclusivity and service. They are firmly located in their denominations and traditions but all are open to share and learn with others. In my encounters with them I recognised a church with discipleship at its core and with a theology and praxis of love. This is a church which gets its sleeves rolled up in communities and recognises the privilege of presence with God's people. It is a church which cherishes humanity. It is a church which can laugh at itself and be serious about mission and grace.

It is my hope that this work will increase the recognition given to women in ministry and encourage women who have not yet pursued their call to do so. I hope that women in ministry will flourish. I hope that, through their diverse ministries, Irish churches and communities will discover a greater hope and wholeness, and move closer to experiencing "life to the full."

Appendix

Questionnaire

INTRODUCTION

I AM CONDUCTING A study into the experience of women in ministry in Ireland (the North and the Republic) and across Christian denominations. This study seeks to collect the views of women whose current main work is Christian ministry and to report on the issues which are important as they engage in ministry at this time. If women are interested there may be a secondary outcome of gathering some women who may wish to meet and discuss their experience (see 3 below).

This work will take place in three stages:

1. Anonymous questionnaire: to gain an overall sense of women's experience and issues which are important to them. This is stage one.

2. Interviews: to have a deeper conversation with some of those who respond from a variety of Christian denominations, ages, experiences. Some or all of these will be anonymous. Some participants may be willing to be identified.

3. Events: one or more events at which women in ministry in Ireland meet and discuss issues which are of shared interest and importance.

The results of this survey will be collated by me, Anne Francis, and will be analysed to inform the second and third stages of the project. Only

I will have access to contact details associated with responses (that is, if I have assistance in recording data any assistant will only see anonymised data). Where I use responses in the final report or publication all responses and personal details will be anonymised.

I intend to publish the results of this research through the Irish Council of Churches; in articles and eventually a book.

Disclaimer I will hold your identity in confidence. No names will be attached to the information you provide. I request that you identify yourself on this form so that I can withdraw your responses from the study should you ask me to do so. You may withdraw from the study at any time by contacting me. In addition, however, you may choose to allow me to contact you for a further discussion. If invited for further discussion, an interview will be conducted with you in person. You will be provided with more information about this and asked to provide your consent at the time. Similarly, you may withdraw at any time, as above.

Updates on the WMI research project can be found on the Women in Ministry in Ireland Facebook page.

My very sincere thanks.

QUESTIONNAIRE

Your name and contact details [optional]:

Name:

Where you live (general area city, county):

E-mail Address:

I understand that my name will be kept confidential for this portion of the research.

I consent to be contacted about the possibility of a further conversation about these matters which may also be anonymous.

My interest in attending a gathering of women in ministry to discuss some of the themes which emerge from stages 1 and 2 of the research.

What key words would you use to describe your ministry (i.e. what do you do?)?

Do you minister within a Christian denomination? If so which one?

Appendix

Are you ordained?

If you are not ordained do you feel called to ordained ministry?

Are you a professed member of a religious order (a sister)?

Are you paid for your work?

Do you have a formal contract of employment?

Do you have other benefits provided by your employer: pension, insurance or other arrangements? If so what are they (broadly)?

How long have you been in Christian ministry as your main life or work choice?

Do you think that your experience of ministry is different to that of male colleagues?

If the answer is 'yes' please indicate the areas in which this is most relevant using these categories where relevant:

- Home
- Ministerial context
- Church structures
- Other

Questionnaire

What, about your ministry, means the most to you?

How is your ministry best supported and nourished?

Who have been role models for you as a minister?

What do you most hope for your ministry in the future?

What do you experience as obstacles in ministry?

As a woman in ministry what two changes would most enhance your experience of ministry?

Please add here any other comments you may have.

Please return this questionnaire to Anne Francis with the subject 'WMI.'

Bibliography

Acheson, Alan. *A History of the Church of Ireland, 1691–2001.* 2nd ed. Dublin: Columba, 2002.

Baillie, Sandra. *Evangelical Women in Belfast: Imprisoned or Empowered?* London: Palgrave Macmillan, 2002.

———. *Presbyterians in Ireland: Identity in the Twenty-First Century.* London: Palgrave Macmillan, 2008.

Brand, Natalie. *Complementarian Spirituality: Reformed Women and Union with Christ.* Eugene, OR: Wipf and Stock, 2013.

Brown, Sally A. "Hermeneutical Theory." In *The Wiley-Blackwell Companion to Practical Theology,* edited by Bonnie Miller-McLemore, 112–22. Chichester, UK: Wiley-Blackwell, 2014.

Church of England. *Living Ministry: Negotiating Wellbeing; Experiences of Ordinands and Clergy in the Church of England.* September 2018. https://www.churchofengland. org/sites/default/files/2018-10/Living%20Ministry%20Qualitative%20Panel%20 Study%20Wave%201%20Report.pdf.

Clear, Catriona. "Walls Within Walls: Nuns in Nineteenth Century Ireland." In *Gender in Irish Society,* edited by Curtin, Chris et al., 134–51. Galway: Galway University Press, 1987.

Concannon, Thomas. *Irish Nuns in Penal Days.* London: Sands, 1931.

Congregation for the Doctrine of the Faith. *The Catechism of the Catholic Church.* Vatican City: Libreria Editrice Vaticana, 1992.

———. *Inter Insigniores: On the Question of Admitting Women to the Ministerial Priesthood.* Vatican City: Libreria Editrice Vaticana, 1976.

Cooney, Dudley L. *The Methodists in Ireland: A Short History.* Dublin: Columba, 2001.

Davies, Douglas. "Practical Theology and Qualitative Research." *Ecclesiology* 5 (2009) 376–78.

Dine, Joy. "God Who Sets Us on a Journey." https://www.methodist.org.uk/our-faith/ worship/singing-the-faith-plus/posts/god-who-sets-us-on-a-journey-website-only/.

Egan, Kevin. *Remaining a Catholic after the Murphy Report.* Dublin: Columba, 2011.

Flannery, Austin, ed. *Vatican II: The Conciliar and Postconciliar Documents.* Dublin: Dominican, 1998.

Fowler, James. *Stages of Faith: The Psychology of Human Development and the Quest for Meaning.* New York: Harper and Rowe, 1981.

Francis, Anne. "Called: Women in Ministry in Ireland 2017." https://www.irishchurches.org/cmsfiles/REPORT-Women-in-Ministry-in-Ireland-Final.pdf.

Gallagher, Sally. *Evangelical Identity and Gendered Family Life.* New Brunswick, NJ: Rutgers University Press, 2003.

Graveling, Elizabeth. "Vocational Pathways: Clergy Leading Larger Churches." April 2016. https://www.churchofengland.org/sites/default/files/2019-08/Vocational%20pathways%20large%20churches.pdf.

Hall, Diane. *Women and the Church in Medieval Ireland, c. 1140–1540.* Dublin: Four Courts, 2003.

Hardy, Jeff. "Only Hours after His Arrival, Pope John Paul II [. . .]" *United Press International*, September 10, 1987. https://www.upi.com/Archives/1987/09/10/Only-hours-after-his-arrival-Pope-John-Paul-II/5227558244800/.

Hempton, David, and Myrtle Hill. *Evangelical Protestantism in Ulster Society, 1740–1890.* London: Routledge, 1992.

———. "Women and Protestant Minorities in Eighteenth Century Ireland." In *Women in Early Modern Ireland*, edited by Margaret MacCurtain et al., 197–221. Edinburgh: Edinburgh University Press, 1991.

Holmes, Janice E. *Religious Revivals in Britain and Ireland, 1859–1905.* Dublin: Irish Academic, 2001.

———. "Women Preachers in the Protestant Churches." In *The Cambridge History of Christianity c1815–1914*, edited by Gilley, Stanley, et al., 84–102. Cambridge: Cambridge University Press, 2014.

Holmes, Janice, and Philippa McCracken. *A Century of Service: Celebrating the Role of Deaconesses in the Church.* Belfast:10Publishing, 2008.

Hayes, Alan, and Diane Urquhart, eds. *The Irish Women's History Reader.* London: Routledge, 2000.

Iona Community. *Dandelions and Thistles: Biblical Meditations from the Iona Community.* Glasgow: Wild Goose, 1999.

Jackson, Thomas, ed. *The Sermons of John Wesley, 1872.* http://wesley.nnu.edu/john-wesley/the-sermons-of-john-wesley-1872-edition/sermon-11-the-witness-of-the-spirit-discourse-two/.

Jarvis, Peter. *The Practitioner-Researcher: Developing Theory from Practice.* San Francisco: Jossey-Bass, 1999.

John Paul II. *Christifideles Laici.* Vatican, 1988.

———. *Familiaris Consortio.* Vatican, 1981.

———. *Mulieris Dignitatem.* Vatican, 1988.

———. *Ordinatio Sacerdotalis.* Vatican, 1994.

Jones, Ian, et al., eds. *Women and Ordination in the Christian Churches: International Perspectives.* Edinburgh: T. & T. Clark, 2011.

Joyce, Kathryn. *Quiverfull: Inside the Christian Patriarchy Movement.* Boston: Beacon, 2009.

Kapalo, James. "Mediating Orthodoxy: Convert Agency and Discursive Autochthonism in Ireland." In *Orthodox Identities in Western Europe*, edited by Maria Hämmerli and Jean Francois Mayer, 229–50. Surrey, UK: Ashgate, 2014.

Karkala-Zorba, Katerina. "The Ordination of Women from an Orthodox Perspective." In *Women and Ordination in the Christian Churches: International Perspectives*, edited by Ian Jones et al., 54–63. Edinburgh: T. & T. Clark, 2011.

Kennerley, Ginnie. *Embracing Women: Making History in the Church of Ireland*. Dublin: Columba, 2008.

Kilroy, Pamela. "Women and the Reformation." In *Women in Early Modern Ireland*, edited by Margaret MacCurtain and Mary O'Dowd, 179–96. Edinburgh: Edinburgh University Press, 1991.

King, Karen L. *The Gospel of Mary of Magdala: Jesus and the First Woman Apostle*. Santa Rosa: Polebridge, 2003.

Larson, Timothy, and Daniel J. Treirer, eds. *The Cambridge Companion to Evangelical Theology*. Cambridge: Cambridge University Press, 2007.

Loades, Ann, ed. *Feminist Theology: A Reader*. London: SPCK, 1990.

Luddy, Maria. *Women and Philanthropy in Nineteenth-Century Ireland*. Cambridge: Cambridge University Press, 1995.

MacCurtain, Margaret, and Mary O'Dowd, eds. *Women in Early Modern Ireland*. Dublin: Wolfhound, 1991.

Macdonald, Sarah. "Pure Codology: The Case for Women Priests." *Irish Independent*, March 31, 2018. https://www.independent.ie/irish-news/pure-codology-the-case-for-women-priests-36758067.html.

Macy, Gary, et al. *Women Deacons: Past, Present and Future*. New Jersey: Paulist, 2011.

Magray, Mary P. *The Transforming Power of the Nuns: Women, Religion and Cultural Change in Ireland, 1750–1900*. Oxford: Oxford University Press, 1998.

Malone, Mary T. *Women and Christianity: From the Reformation to the Twenty-First Century*. Dublin: Columba 2003.

———. *Women and Christianity: The First Thousand Years*. Dublin: Columba, 2000.

———. *Women and Christianity: The Medieval Period, AD 1000–1500*. Dublin: Columba 2001.

McAleese, Martin, et al. "Report of the Inter-Departmental Committee to Establish the Facts of State Involvement with the Magdalen Laundries." Department of Justice, Ireland. February 2013. http://www.justice.ie/en/JELR/Pages/MagdalenRpt2013.

McAleese, Mary. "The Time Is Now for Change in the Catholic Church." Voices of Faith International Women's Day Conference, Jesuit Curia, Rome, March 8, 2018. https://static1.squarespace.com/static/5a28981618b27d9cb5404470/t/5abda1bc758d46a7b6196e77/1522377151258/VoicesofFaithmarymcaleesetext+copy.pdf.

McKenna, Yvonne. *Made Holy: Irish Women Religious at Home and Abroad*. Dublin: Irish Academic, 2006.

Megahey, Alan, J. *The Irish Protestant Churches in the Twentieth Century*. London: Palgrave MacMillan, 2000.

Methodist Church in Ireland. *The Constitution of the Methodist Church in Ireland*. 1927. https://static1.squarespace.com/static/604f6c4cbaa61721597a264b/t/60b4f4aa4befde1ce956853d/1622471850324/The+Constitution+of+the+Methodist+Church+in+Ireland.pdf.

Meyers, Carol, ed. *Women in Scripture: A Dictionary of Named and Unnamed Women in the Hebrew Bible, the Aprochryphal/Deuterocanonical Books, and the New Testament*. Grand Rapids: Eerdmans, 2000.

Miller-McLemore, Bonnie, ed. *The Wiley-Blackwell Companion to Practical Theology*. Chichester, UK: Wiley-Blackwell, 2014.

Molina, Noelia. "Religious Vocations in Ireland: Challenges and Opportunities." Research project on behalf of Vocations Ireland. October 2017. http://www.vocationsireland. com/research-religious-vocations-in-ireland-challenges-and-opportunities/.

O'Brien, Susan. *Leaving God for God: The Daughters of Charity of St Vincent de Paul in Britain, 1847–2017*. London: DLT, 2017.

O'Dowd, Mary. *A History of Women in Ireland, 1500–1800*. Harlow: Pearson Education, 2005.

Osiek Carolyn, et al. *A Woman's Place: House Churches in Earliest Christianity*. Minneapolis: Fortress, 2005.

Osmer, Richard R. *Practical Theology: An Introduction*. Grand Rapids, Michigan: Eerdmans, 2008.

Paul VI. *Octogesima Adveniens*. Vatican, 1971

———. *Perfectae Caritatis*. Vatican, 1965.

———. *Women in the Plan of God*. Vatican,1977.

Pietkiewicz, Igor, and Jonathon Smith. "A Practical Guide to Using Interpretative Phenomenological Analysis in Qualitative Research Psychology." *Psychological Journal* 18 (2012) 361–69.

The Presbyterian Church of Ireland. "The Code: Constitution and Government of the Presbyterian Church in Ireland." 1979. http://www.presbyterianireland.org/ Resources/General-Assembly/The-Code.aspx.

———. "The History of Presbyterian Women." http://www.presbyterianireland.org/pw/ History-of-PW.aspx.

Prior Smaby, Beverly. "Moravian Women during the Eighteenth Century." http:// zinzendorf.com/pages/index.php?id=moravian-women.

Radford Ruether, Rosemary. *Sexism and God-Talk: Towards a Feminist Theology*. London: SCM, 1983.

Raughter, Rosemary, ed. *Religious Women and Their History: Breaking the Silence*. Dublin: Irish Academic, 2005.

Regan, M. Joanna, and Isabelle Keiss. *Tender Courage*. Chicago: Franciscan Herald, 1988.

Research and Development Unit of the Catholic Communications Institute of Ireland. "Survey of Catholic Clergy and Religious Personnel, 1971." *Social Studies / Irish Journal of Sociology* 1 (1972) 137–234.

Robbins, Amanda. "The Cost of a Calling: Clergywomen and Work in the Church of England." *Gender, Work and Organization* 22 (2015) 405–20.

Robbins, Mandy, and Anne-Marie Greene. "Clergywomen's Experience of Ministry in the Church of England." *Journal of Gender Studies* 27 (2018) 890–900.

Rohr, Richard. *Falling Upward: A Spirituality for the Two Halves of Life*. San Francisco: Jossey-Bass, 2011.

Ross, Susan. *Extravagant Affections: A Feminist Sacramental Theology*. London: Continuum, 1998.

Ryan, Seán. "The Report of the Commission to Inquire into Child Abuse" (The Ryan Report). 2009. http://www.childabusecommission.ie/rpt/pdfs/.

Schussler Fiorenza, Elizabeth. "The Apostleship of Women in Early Christianity." In *Women Priests: A Catholic Commentary on the Vatican Declaration*, edited by Leonard J. Swidler and Arlene Swidler, 135–40. New York: Paulist, 1977.

———. *In Memory of Her: A Feminist Theological Reconstruction of Christian Origins*. London: SCM, 1983.

Smith, Jonathan A., et al. *Interpretative Phenomenological Analysis: Theory, Method and Research*. London: Sage, 2009.

Sophia Network. "Women in the Church: Experiences, Barriers and Hopes." Minding the Gap Research Project, 2018. https://kyrianetwork.com/minding-the-gap/.

Stackhouse, John G. *Partners in Christ: A Conservative Case for Egalitarianism.* Downers Grove: InterVarsity, 2015.

Storkey, Elaine. "Gender and Evangelical Theology." In *The Cambridge Companion to Evangelical Theology*, edited by Timothy Larsen and Daniel J. Treier, 161–75. Cambridge: Cambridge University Press, 2007.

Swinton, John, and Harriet Mowat. *Practical Theology and Qualitative Research.* 2nd ed. London: SCM, 2016.

Tashakkori, Abbas, and Charles Teddlie, eds. *The Sage Handbook of Mixed Methods in Social and Behavioural Research.* 2nd ed. London: Sage, 2010.

Therese of Lisieux. *Journal of a Soul: Autobiography of St. Therese of Lisieux.* Christian Classic Ethereal Library. https://d2y1pz2y630308.cloudfront.net/2232/documents/2018/5/The%20Story%20of%20a%20Soul.pdf.

Thomas, Gabriel. "Receiving the Gift: Using Receptive Ecumenism to Explore Women's Experiences of Working within Diverse Churches in England." June 2019. https://www.durham.ac.uk/media/durham-university/research-/research-centres/catholic-studies-centre-for-ccs/Women-and-the-Churches-Shorter-Report-compressed.pdf.

Trible, Phyllis. *God and the Rhetoric of Sexuality: Overtures to Biblical Theology.* Philadelphia: Fortress, 1986.

Valiulis, Maryann G., and Mary O'Dowd, eds. *Women and Irish History.* Dublin: Wolfhound, 1997.

Victorin-Vangerud, Nancy. *The Raging Hearth: Spirit in the Household of God.* St. Louis: Chalice, 2000.

Walsh, Oonagh. "Protestant Female Philanthropy in Dublin in the Early 20th Century." *History Ireland* 5 (1997) 27–31. http://www.historyireland.com/20th-century-contemporary-history/protestant-female-philanthropy-in-dublin-in-the-early-20th-century/.

Walsh, T. J. *Nano Nagle and the Presentation Sisters.* Dublin: Gill, 1959.

Watts, Donald. J. "Letter from Clerk of the General Assembly to All Clergy of the Presbyterian Church in Ireland." January 25, 2008. Full text available at http://www.bbc.co.uk/blogs/ni/2008/02/will_presbyterians_ever_elect.html.

Wesley, John. "Sermon XI: The Witness of the Spirit." 1872. http://wesley.nnu.edu/john-wesley/the-sermons-of-john-wesley-1872-edition/sermon-11-the-witness-of-the-spirit-discourse-two/.

Wijngaards, John. *The Ordination of Women in the Catholic Church: Unmasking a Cuckoo's Egg Tradition.* London: Darton, Longman & Todd, 2001.

Winter, Miriam T. *Out of the Depths: The Story of Ludmila Javorova, Ordained Roman Catholic Priest.* New York: Crossroads, 2001.

Women and the Church (WATCH). "WATCH Launches Report on the Developments in Women's Ministry in 2016." https://womenandthechurch.org/news/watch-developments-womens-ministry-2016/.

Zagano, Phyllis. *Women & Catholicism: Gender, Communion, and Authority.* New York: Palgrave Macmillan, 2011.

———, ed. *Women Deacons? Essays with Answers.* Wilmington, DE: Glazier, 2016.

———. *Women Deacons: Past, Present, Future.* New York: Paulist, 2012.

Printed in Great Britain
by Amazon

58009034R00096